The Confident portExplorer

by Cathy Rogers

For Penny
with many happy
memories
and all
best wishes

Cathy Rogers.

Published by JJ Moffs Independent Book Publisher 2018

JJMoffs Independent Book Publisher Ltd
Grove House Farm, Grovewood Road,
Misterton, Nottinghamshire DN10 4EF

Typeset by Anna Richards
Cover by The Brand Pharmacy

Contents

INTRODUCTION

You might be wondering why you need a specialist book about planning your time ashore on a cruise holiday. After all, you travel for leisure, or maybe business, and you're perfectly capable of sorting out a holiday, so why would a cruise be any different?

Of course, the simple answer is that it isn't exactly different, as you need to do the same sort of planning and preparation that you would do for any holiday. It is just that on a one-week cruise you are going to need to do that planning as many as five or six times and, as each port will present you with a different challenge, it can become a bit like planning five holidays at once! This book is written to help you make a few important decisions, sort through all the different choices, and put together your perfect cruise experience.

It was a cruise to the Baltic that sparked the idea that eventually became portExplore. I love travelling – everything about it – particularly guidebooks and maps, which meant that this was a really good excuse to hit the shops and stock up. Copenhagen, Stockholm, Tallinn, Helsinki, St. Petersburg, Warnemunde... Six different ports, six different countries, six different books! And then it turned out that those books were pretty useless. They were full of things that I didn't need, such as where to stay, where to have dinner, nightclubs, theatres, ferry connections – all sorts of irrelevant information. Yet they managed to omit all the things that I actually needed to know, such as where would the ship dock? Could we walk into town from there?

Where was the train station? Their maps didn't even show the Cruise Port where the ship would dock!

That's when I knew that cruise passengers needed something more targeted and relevant for a traveller with potentially as little as seven hours to explore a new city, especially when that city was in a country with a completely different language and currency to the place they were in yesterday. So that is where the idea for this book was born. It has been written to give you the resources to find the information you need, to help you make the most of your time ashore. Remember, great cruises don't just happen, you need to plan them. This book will help you do just that.

CHAPTER 1

WHERE, WHEN, HOW –
BEFORE YOU BOOK A CRUISE

The first three things to consider when you begin to plan a cruise are the itinerary, the ship, and the cruise line; it is almost the cruise equivalent of 'which came first, the chicken or the egg?'. The price will factor in as well obviously, but before you can compare prices, you need to know what it is that you want to do. Everyone you speak to will have a different opinion about which is most important when planning a perfect cruise and you will soon learn what your own priorities are, but in reality, all three choices inform each other. So you need to start by imagining your perfect cruise, see what is important to you and things should start to become clearer. Let's consider each variable in turn.

ITINERARY

The first question about the itinerary is basically 'where do you want to go?' although the answer to that question will have to depend on the time of year that you want to travel. Unlike air travel you can only cruise to a destination during its **cruise season**, for example, the Alaskan Season starts in late April and finishes in September, so there is no point attempting to plan a trip there in February. Sometimes the time you have available to travel will dictate your destination, other times you have a long-held dream to go to a particular place and will plan around that, often you just fall across a really good deal. If you have restricted holiday available to you, or your plans are constrained by dates, then find out what destinations are available at that time of year in order to make a decision. If you are planning further ahead, or have a long-held dream to visit somewhere in particular, then find out the best times of year to visit.

For me, where the ship is heading is my first priority. I usually have a **'bucket list'** of three or four places that I really want to visit, so when I can get some time away I look to see which areas are available on those dates, then I bump those destinations to the top of my list, especially if I see a particularly good deal! Once you have a destination in mind, take a very close look at a map because Cruise Companies can be very naughty and quite often label a big industrial deep water port as its nearest, must-see iconic location in their itinerary. The word that you need to watch out for is **'FOR'** as you will see, for example, Le Havre, France labelled as 'for Paris', Civittavechia, Italy labelled 'for Rome' and Laem Chabang, Thailand 'for Bangkok. You will find that FOR often means an expensive transfer and a long day away from the ship. We will talk about this in more detail later, but at this point the most important thing you need to consider is, if what you actually want to do more than anything else is visit Paris, then booking a weekend trip might be a better option than booking a cruise that will dock over two hours drive away for less than half a day's visit!

If you have dreams of a 'must see' destination then make sure before you book your cruise, that you will get to spend a reasonable amount of time there.

If you have a really good list of destinations that you are hoping to visit, occasionally you can kill two birds with one stone, as well as get an excellent deal, by booking a **repositioning cruise**. This is the name the cruise industry gives to the voyage at the end of the season when the cruise line relocates its ships to the next season's home base. They tend to be longish cruises with a lot of sea days but are worth considering because you get the opportunity to visit two completely different regions in one cruise. An example; Caribbean cruises are often based out of Miami for the winter, in the Spring there will be a **transatlantic** repositioning cruise to maybe Barcelona or Southampton ready for their summer season in the Mediterranean, then in late Autumn the ships will travel in the opposite direction. For a couple of years now I have been keeping my eye on a Princess cruise line repositioning that takes you from Hong Kong to Alaska via Japan. That would tick off some dream destinations for me, but unfortunately, the timings have not been quite right yet, maybe one day! The downside of repositioning cruises is that they are usually more than a couple of weeks long, plus the weather can be a bit unpredictable because it will be the edge of the tourist season in both destinations. The upside is that the price is often very good value, and the crew is usually in a party mood because they are reaching the end of their season's contract. If you have the time, it's a pretty good way to have an excellent long holiday and is much better value than a similar length sector of a World Cruise.

Let's assume that you have decided where and when you want to go and you are looking to see what is available. This is where the **size of ship** comes into the equation for various reasons. The newest 'mega' ships have space for nearly 5000 passengers; smaller ships can carry as few as 500. Obviously the bigger the ship, the more cabins will be available, so the more likely it is that there will be some good deals on offer. On the other hand the bigger the ship, the fewer ports it can actually dock in, so the destinations that it can visit will be restricted, and you may not get the island experience you are dreaming of.

Large **Industrial Ports** are usually situated in part of a container port and sited well away from the nearest town. Hamburg or Zeebrugge are good examples. You may not even be able to leave the ship on foot as heightened security will often mean that you have to use a Shuttle Bus just to get you to the port gate. These ports can be quite ugly, certainly not picturesque, and are often quite inaccessible.

Deep Water Ports, particularly those situated basically in the town such as Bergen or Naples are usually best, as even the biggest ships can get alongside. You can walk straight off the ship and into town without the need for shuttles, transfers, or taxis.

If a ship can't dock alongside (i.e. tied up on the shore), either because of its size or because of port restrictions, it is called a **Tender Port**. The ship will moor outside the harbour and use tenders (small boats - usually the lifeboats) to transfer passengers ashore, normally to a conveniently located position in the town. This is not a quick operation and will always lose you time that could otherwise be spent ashore. Cruise companies prefer to avoid them as they cause a lot of extra work for the crew and can be a real problem in rough weather as they are the most likely ports to be cancelled at the last minute. It is not always clear when you are at the booking stage if a port will be a tender call – it should be marked, usually with an anchor sign – but it is often not clear enough so do some homework before booking if this is important to you and particularly if you have impaired movement or vision as **disability access** to tenders is very limited and can be quite trying (for example many ships do not allow mobility scooters on tenders.) Don't forget that whether it is a tender port or not may vary between size of ship; Fred Olsen's 'Balmoral', with 1700 passengers, is able to get alongside at Port Leith, Edinburgh whereas the RCI Symphony of the Seas, with its 5000+ guests, would not. She would have to 'moor off' at Port Rosyth where guests would be tendered ashore for their 40 minute drive into the city.

TOP TIP

Use Google maps (or an atlas!) to see where the ports are and how far the cruise actually travels. You can also get a satellite view of the ports in relation to the town which all helps build a picture of the holiday on offer and is worth checking before you book. I once had someone say they were disappointed by the number of sea days there were; they were on a ship heading from New York to Southampton. I'm not sure they had ever actually looked to see how far it really is or if they had always been really poor at geography!

When you start to compare cruises, you will begin to see the difference between the ships doing them. The largest ships will list only ports in big, well-known cities such as Barcelona, Rome, Athens, Venice - whereas smaller ships may offer Mykonos, Argosteli, Santorini, Rhodes. You start to get a feel for the ship size by the port names that you are seeing, and if you look at a place name and say "where?!", it's probably a very small expedition ship, such as Celebrities 'X class' ships, that cruise the Galapagos.

CRUISE LINE

For many people, the actual cruise line itself is the driving factor and they will decide on this first before considering where the ship is going; people can be very loyal and stick with one ship or a particular company (or group of companies) for years. Cruisers can be very protective of 'their' cruise line; you only have to spend a bit of time on online cruise forums to see that! To be fair, staying loyal to one cruise company can definitely have its advantages as they all run **loyalty schemes** which could eventually give you onboard credit, free wifi, and other perks, as well as invitations to special events onboard. If you have enjoyed your time on a cruise, it might make sense to travel with the same company again and build up some loyalty points (and if you decide to book your next cruise whilst still onboard that can get you some good deals too). I cover the different cruise lines and both their loyalty schemes and their future cruise bonuses in more detail in *The Confident Cruiser,* which is more focused on the ships and cruise lines and less on the

INTERESTING FACT!

The most popular perk at sea is the unlimited laundry and dry-cleaning for Princess Elite and Suites passengers - seriously! This is a hugely valued freebie and apparently, some guests actually arrive on board with dirty laundry packed in their suitcase!

destinations and what to do when you get there. Take a look at the various schemes but generally I would say that they are not normally a good reason on their own to book a particular cruise.

Staying with a cruise line that you have enjoyed may sound a little repetitive but, as the old saying goes, the grass is not always greener elsewhere. Everyone you talk to will have an opinion, but before you take their recommendation, you need to know that they like similar things to you. This is where a specialist **cruise travel agent** can help, they will have a broad knowledge of the different companies and should be able to point you in the direction of a cruise line that you will like. The quickest way to check for yourself is to take a really good look at the facilities offered onboard. The larger the ship, the more facilities it will have, such as waterparks or ice skating rinks, and a quick look at onboard activities may set off some alarm bells for you - Afternoon tea dance? Street parties? String quartets? Foam parties in the pool? Ballroom dancing? All-inclusive drinks? Kids clubs? Although I admit that there are some cruise lines that I would never, ever consider (either 'at all' or 'ever again'!) the cruise company that I book with is probably my least important consideration, with the itinerary and ship size most important. That's my view; now you need to think hard, investigate your choices and decide on what matters most to you for this holiday.

STILL MORE DECISIONS

Once you've made those choices, you still have a few more to think about. You may feel proud to have deleted all the emails about Alaskan Cruises or chucked out the P&O Brochures, you may even be down to a much smaller group of options that all include Athens in September, but now you need to do even more soul-searching. Really drilling down and thinking about what you want from your cruise at this stage should pay dividends and save you from unexpected scenarios or disappointments later.

So, let's say you know when and where you want to go, the size of ship, and which cruise lines you might consider. Maybe you're looking at a two-week cruise with five ports. Now that immediately tells us that you will have as many as nine days spent completely at sea. Does that sound about right? Or does it sound as if there is not enough time ashore? **Sea days** are another issue that completely divides cruisers. Personally, I love them and will happily spend time sitting on deck watching the sea pass by. To me, a couple of sea days, book-ending the holiday with the first and last day spent at sea is perfect, although I'm happy to spend more time at sea on a repositioning voyage. Other people want to avoid sea days completely if possible, preferring to visit a new place every day, spending just evenings aboard.

If you are new to cruising, I suggest you choose a fairly balanced cruise, maybe four ports in seven days, and see what you consider to be the perfect balance between the two. Just to be clear though, the one thing that sea days are not is boring! There are so many different things going on that you would never be able to do them all and again in *The Confident Cruiser*, there is loads more information about how to plan your perfect day at sea.

FLY-CRUISE

If you want to reduce the number of sea days, for example, while the ship is 'making' passage' to your destination then you should board your ship close to the area that you will be cruising in. As an example; for a fortnights cruise in the Mediterranean you could join the ship in Southampton, spend three days steaming south towards the Mediterranean, see six ports over the next eight days and then spend another three travelling back to the UK, or you could join the ship in Barcelona, visit nine or ten ports in the next two weeks and get off again, maybe in Barcelona or even somewhere completely different.

Therefore, the best way to avoid the 'at sea' section of the journey, which also means that you may avoid rougher seas and weather, is to take a flight at the beginning and end of the cruise. A **fly-cruise**, as it is known, gets you off on your holiday quicker. Three hours from the UK and you are looking at the sun shining on the Med, eight hours and you are in the Caribbean, twelve hours and you are boarding a ship in Singapore. That is not to say you shouldn't consider joining your cruise ship close to your **home port** as it has big advantages, the main ones being that you can take as much luggage as you like with no weight restrictions, your journey to port is more predictable and less liable to delay, and most importantly that you can literally park your car, or step out of the coach or taxi, someone will take your luggage and you will be 'on holiday' within thirty minutes! (We once checked in to Queens Grill on Cunard, found our suite, unpacked and wandered up to find lunch. After a lovely meal in a sunny courtyard, where we made friends over a glass of wine with a charming couple at the next table, I looked up as the coffee arrived and was genuinely surprised to find that we were still in Southampton!). Some people hate flying, some cannot fly for health reasons and others just don't want the hassle, so you tend to find a slightly wider age group on a cruise from Southampton than you will on a fly-cruise.

The main implications of flying are the additional cost and time (bear in mind that you will probably have to extend your holiday by at least a day). If possible book the flight through the cruise line as you are then under their care as soon as you check in. They may have chartered a plane for the cruise or you may be on a scheduled flight but either way, although you will be subject to the normal restrictions on what you can pack and luggage weight, if there is any flight delay or a problem of any sort, the cruise line will be responsible for getting you to the ship (even if it has moved on to its next port). A cruise line will normally fly you out the day before the cruise and put you up overnight in a hotel, so this won't be an issue and obviously, it also gives you another days holiday with either some time to sightsee before joining the ship or possibly just to be one of the first to board. If you have had a long flight then staying a night or two beforehand will help reduce the effect of **jet lag**, meaning you are less likely to spend the first day of your cruise fast asleep! If you decide to book your own flights, then it is even more important to plan to arrive the day before, because missing the cruise due to **flight delay** will not be covered by travel insurance and you will have to catch the ship up at the next port at your own expense. When booking a cruise always ask for a price including a flight booked through the cruise line and compare with the DIY cost. Don't forget that even if Air Miles or budget airlines flights might initially seem cheaper, when you add in all transfers, overnight stays and luggage costs, it may not be much more expensive to have the complete peace of mind that you get with flights booked through the cruise company. In addition, your main luggage will usually be transferred to the ship separately, so that once you've checked it in at the airport, you won't see it again until it arrives at your cabin door.

If you are taking a really long flight, to Singapore for example, for a Far East cruise, then I would make the most of it by adding both a pre and post cruise hotel. You can get some very good deals through the cruise companies and airlines as they will have access to prices that you do not! It is really worth considering this otherwise you could to take a cruise to Hong Kong and not really see it at all. If your flight times are against you then there may only be time to transfer to the airport and **fly home**. In my view, you really do want to see more of your final port than just the inside of the airport!

FINAL DECISIONS

Before finally booking a cruise, I would always want to see a **detailed itinerary** with estimated arrival and departure times so that you can to double check your choices before finally handing over your deposit.

Double check:
How many ports and how many sea days? Are you happy with the balance?
Are there any overnight stops in port? Are there two ports shown for one day?

You might like to check what **other ships** are in port on the same day as yours at www.cruisetimetables.com. It isn't going to be a deal breaker at this point but it is handy information. If there are four other cruise ships in port on the same day as you then there will be pressure on local tours, taxis and car hire for any excursions you want to plan. This will let you know that you should get on and book them promptly. Cruisetimetables is also a good website for checking information on individual ports, even more importantly you can even create yourself a personalised 'Countdown to my cruise' which is quite fun!

DETAILS

At this point, I would just quickly check some **details**. I wouldn't be expecting to find anything that stopped me from booking, but it is sensible to have up to date information. Take a quick look at official advice about **security** in the area and check if you will need any **visas** on www.gov.uk/foreign-travel-advice; also you can see if you will need any **vaccinations** on www.fitfortravel.nhs.uk/destinations. Remember to check ALL the countries that you will be visiting. Take a quick look at your **passport** as it will need to be valid for at least six months after your visit in most countries. Crucially you must also put **travel insurance** in place at this point, make sure it specifically covers cruises. We will revisit all of this again in the chapter on **PLANNING,** but it's just good to be aware before you book of things that could give you concern you later.

Itinerary, ship, cruise line, price, transport, details... All checked, discussed and decided - BOOK IT!

CHAPTER 2

PLOTTING AND PLANNING
TURNING AN ITINERARY INTO REALITY

Your cruise is booked – now you just have to organise everything else, it is time for a bit of serious plotting and planning!

YOU NEED A SYSTEM!

You will amass a huge pile of information at this stage; I find the best way to keep it all under control is a notebook/checklist/expanding wallet **planning system**. I use the notebook to keep a physical list of what has been done and what is left to do, effectively an overview of the whole cruise. An expanding wallet with a section for each port/hotel/flight etc. is somewhere to store the myriad of printouts, tickets, and information that you need to keep. I have a **master checklist** for the cruise (see page 18) and separate checklists for each port (see Chapter 6) which I fix to the front of A4 envelopes, transferring all the information from the wallet when we are getting ready to go, and packing both the envelopes and the notebook. Obviously in 'real life' we are used to keeping a lot of this sort of information online or in 'cloud' storage (I also like to use the Tripit App) but **internet** connections onboard are often expensive, slow, and unreliable so it really is best to have hard copies of important information printed out before you go - although I also have most important documents saved as PDF on my phone so that I can access them without internet if necessary. You will normally be able to access 4G through **data roaming** when you are ashore (check costs with your call provider), but as soon as the ship heads to sea you will need to pay for internet services; these will be connected via a satellite signal through the ships Wi-Fi, which is usually painfully slow and very expensive. Waiting until you get ashore is not a good plan, we once waited nearly half an hour with our privately guided group, for someone to find a WiFi hotspot in order to open their email and find the relevant booking confirmation number for our guide. They were not popular – please don't be that person! It may feel dated, but paper can sometimes be the simplest thing.

YOUR CRUISE PERSONALISER

Shortly after booking your cruise, your cruise line (not your travel agent if you used one) will send you details for their **cruise personaliser**. You will need the booking number on your confirmation documents to access it. The personaliser has many functions; there will be an advance passenger information section that you will need to complete, as well as sections where you can make excursion, spa, and restaurant bookings. This is also where you can make pre-cruise purchases of various drinks and celebration packages – but what we are interested in here is getting some real detail about your cruise, so log in now and take a look (this is also the time to sign up for the loyalty points scheme of the cruise line if you are not already a member.)

The section of the Personaliser that we want will probably be labelled **ship's itinerary** or Ship's Calendar.

MASTER CHECKLIST

Cruise: _____

Cruise Number: _____

Cruiseline: _____

Dates: _____

Ship: _____

Booking Ref: _____

Agent name/number: _____

Website: _____

Cabin Number: _____

Deck: _____

Loyalty Membership No./ level:

_____

CRUISE PERSONALISER

Login Details: _____

Passenger Information completed: _____

Bookings made: _____

Packages ordered: _____

FLIGHTS

Airline: _____

OUT Airport: _____ Flight No: _____

Depart: _____ Arrive: _____

RTN Airport: _____ Flight No: _____

Depart: _____ Arrive: _____

Airline Login: _____

Loyalty No: _____

Passport Info Completed:

Out _____ Rtn _____

SEATS RESERVED:

Out _____ Rtn _____

CHECKED IN:

Out _____ Rtn _____

VISA required flight?: _____

Transport to ship/ airport: _____

Parking @ Port / Airport: _____

Transfers Booked: _____

Hotel(s): _____

Contact info: _____

It contains a more detailed itinerary than you will have had when booking and is our starting point for your plans. It will show clearly on which day of the cruise you will arrive at each port and how long you will stay there – bear in mind that occasionally you will find an overnight stop in port which will give you more time to explore as well as the opportunity for an evening ashore. Do not assume that any anomaly in the itinerary is a mistake, especially in relation to the actual timings, as these will NOT be the same at every port and both arrival and departure times will vary. **Never assume** anything on a cruise, always check and be sure! Factors that will influence the time you are scheduled to spend in a port will include the ideal timings for the cruise line's main excursions, the variety of tours that the ship can offer, and the distance the ship has to travel to the next port. For example, on a 'Baltic' cruise the main destination is St Petersburg where the ship will normally stay overnight. This gives the opportunity for excursions to be spread over two days with the additional option of an evening trip to the theatre, maybe to see the Ballet, Opera, or Folk show.

I need to say at this point that the most important thing you need to know about planning ahead on a cruise is that you can only do so much. You have to **stay flexible** because things can change; the timings you see are the **intended** times of arrival and departure, but poor weather or other problems may alter or even prevent them altogether. If you suffer a **missed port** it can be very disappointing, and tempers can get very frayed, but there is nothing you can do. The Captain has the final say on the safety of both passengers and ship, and if he is not prepared to take a ship into port or if he feels that poor weather will make the use of tenders too dangerous, he will cancel that stop. There will be no point haranguing the Excursion Desk staff about it as once the decision has been made it will be final. Any tours booked through the cruise company will be automatically refunded, and normally those booked through external companies who specialise in cruise excursions will be too – you may wish to check this when booking. Other bookings that you might have made, such as car hire or entrance tickets, may not be refundable but should be covered by your cruise travel insurance, so check that you have 'missed port cover' in your policy. The one thing that would not be covered is your disappointment, and this is why you need to understand that it could happen, particularly with a tender port. As an example, the Falkland Islands are an important stop on a South American cruise, and for many British passengers, it is the destination that they most want to see. Unfortunately, because it is a tender port with very unpredictable weather, a large proportion of cruises (unofficially I have heard that it is more than 50%) headed there don't actually dock. A holiday at sea is less predictable than a holiday on land, but that's all part of the fun!

'WHOLE CRUISE' PLANNING

The Cruise Itinerary then, gives information on sea days, port arrivals, and departures. Reading it will enable you to see the overall 'arc' of the voyage so that you can begin to plan what you will do in each port. On a cruise that is covering five ports over a week or so it can be easy to overdo things and get a little jaded. Four full-day excursions to see Greek and Roman temples in searing heat over four consecutive days may well be one too many! Remember, the excursions you see in the Personaliser are not all there is to do in port, there are many other options and sometimes it's just nice to spend a day at the beach!

Overleaf you will see an actual cruise that I have chosen to use as an example throughout the book so that as we talk about the planning, you will be able to see how it all builds up. It was downloaded from the Cruise Personaliser, and then the information in **bold** was added by me. I do this because it is very easy to lose track of what day it actually is when you are on a cruise. Also, although every day on board is much the same, it can make a big difference to what will be happening, or even open, ashore and affect what you are able to do. In a city, traffic will be worse on a weekday, especially at the end of the working day. On a Sunday in a small port it may be that only 'touristy' things are open; alternatively it might turn out to be Market day and then spending it mooching around town might seem more fun than visiting a famous battlefield two hours away! Museums, tourist sights, art galleries, etc. will all have days that they close, especially in low season.

I usually check on timeanddate.com and add the **sunrise & sunset** times to my chart. This is less important for summer cruises, (although it is fun to see the times for June in the Baltic!) but especially worth doing on winter cruises when in the Northern hemisphere (vice versa in the Southern hemisphere) when it can get dark quite early in the day as you will see below.

Day	Date	Port	Arrive	Depart	Sunrise	Sunset
Day 1	S11	Civittavechia, Rome, Italy	17.00		16.53	
Day 2	M12	Catania, Sicily Italy	14.00	20.00		16.51
Day 3	T13	At sea				
Day 4	W14	Piraeus, Athens, Greece	6.00	16.00	7.04	17.14
Day 5	T15	Suez Canal passage	23.00			
Day 6	F16	Suez Canal passage		13.00		
Day 7	S17	Aqaba, Jordan	8.00	20.00	6.05	16.43
Day 8	S18	At sea				
Day 9	M19	At sea				
Day 10	T20	At sea				
Day 11	W21	At sea				
Day 12	T22	At sea				
Day 13	F23	Muscat Oman	10.00	16.00	6.25	17.18
Day 14	S24	Abu Dhabi UAE	16.00			19.14
Day 15	S25	Abu Dhabi UAE				19.14
Day 16	M26	Abu Dhabi UAE		9.00	5.36	

As you can see this was a 'repositioning' cruise going from Civittavechia, Italy, which had been the ship's Mediterranean home for the summer, to the Middle Eastern base of Abu Dhabi for the winter season. In comparison to a more normal week-long cruise schedule it has an unusually gentle arc; 16 days, 5 ports, 7 full sea days, 2 half sea days, 2 overnights in port, and a transit through the Suez Canal. The canal was an important factor for us when booking the cruise, and we had long wanted to see Petra, Jordan which is accessed from Aqaba on the Red Sea. We are also fans of the film The Godfather and the TV series Inspector Montalbano set in Sicily, so we thought we might hire a car and do a little location spotting. We had been to Athens before, and so had no real thoughts about what we wanted to do there. We didn't really know anything about Muscat, but straight away we realised that we would be there on a Friday and so not able to visit a Mosque. The two overnights in Abu Dhabi seemed odd, but we found out that it was because the ship's visit coincided with the Grand Prix so we needed to decide what to do about that as it would probably impinge on normal sightseeing that weekend.

This is where you need to think about the pace of your holiday. In this case, the number of sea days meant that we didn't need to avoid planning two busy days back to back, but the late arrival time and the early sunset in Sicily meant that the car hire idea for Catania was a non-starter. We also realised that it would be dark quite early in Jordan and that when we arrived in Athens, we could have a lie in as although the ship arrived at 6.00 it would be dark for another hour! This is the sort of thing to think about as you plan the holiday overall and each port individually. Take some time to decide what you really want from this cruise. Are you a traveller who will want to squeeze the most out of every minute ashore, or do you want a laid back holiday with a bit of sightseeing? Lots of culture, or a long trek with a bit of white water rafting? It's probably worth having a discussion with your travel companions at this point so that everyone considers their preference for the relaxation/sightseeing split and puts in a vote for the things that they consider really important to see in any one particular place (on one visit to Molde in Norway this turned out to be a football stadium!)

Port/Country	Ships Excursions	Thoughts
Catania, Sicily, Italy	Taormina	Maybe, quite a way? Or Mount Etna? only 3 hours light
Piraeus, Athens, Greece	Acropolis	Been before. Maybe DIY metro into town ??
Aqaba, Jordan	Petra	YES
Muscat Oman	City Tour walking or boat trip	Not sure. Can we get to desert?? We will have been at sea 5 days!
Abu Dhabi UAE	Grand Mosque Desert tour	Or the Grand Prix!

A good starting point for planning your '**must sees**' at any given port is the list of ship's tours in the personaliser. This is not an exhaustive list of everything you can do in that port, it is only the guided excursions that are available from the ship, but it will help you work out what the cruise company considers the 'must see' destinations in each port – and then you can decide if they matter to you.

These are the highlight tours on our example cruise and our initial thoughts about them: Once you know what the main options are you can start to investigate **what else** is available in each port and what else you might want to do. As a general rule cruise excursions tend to avoid smaller attractions that would be swamped by a large group of tourists pouring out from three coaches! Remember; they are selling you an experience not promising that they will tell you about the best one for you! It's not just what is popular locally either; you might have a specific interest in a particular place. Maybe you read a book or watched a film that was set there. Location spotting can be a great basis for a DIY walking tour. Was a famous artist, musician, or composer born locally? For example, *Troldhaugen*, the house where Norwegian Composer Greig lived for most of his life, is open to visitors alongside a stunning new concert hall with daily lunchtime recitals, a museum, and a restaurant. It does not feature on the cruise excursion lists for Bergen, but you can get there on a free bus from the tourist information office! So spend some time finding out what sort of other things are nearby, don't just check specialist cruise excursion companies look at other sources too. Trip Advisor is always good, Youtube will have information videos, and obviously look at the local tourist information sites.

Work on ONE PORT AT A TIME, or you will get confused! Decide which, if any, of the 'must do's' you actually want to do, choose the most important port first; in our example that was Aqaba for Petra. So plan that day first and then decide what you want to do on other days. That way you can take control of the pace of your holiday.

If you feel that a long day will be tiring you could plan to follow it with a shorter, less strenuous day; or you might feel that after six hours sitting on a coach one day, you would prefer something a bit more energetic the next. If nothing immediately appeals then leave that port blank for now, something will come up later. Leaving a bit of space for spontaneity is always a good move.

CHAPTER 3

DIGGING DEEPER
STARTING TO PLAN WHAT YOU WANT TO DO

So you now have a cruise booked and it's time to get a general idea about where you are going and what might be good options for your port days. You have the opportunity now for a bit more thought and planning before final decisions have to be made; unless you are going on your cruise fairly soon the more time you take checking things out before you go, the better the time you are going to have - there is no need to book the first thing you see.

RECAP

This book is really focused on planning your time ashore, you will find much more about planning related to the actual cruise in The Confident Cruiser but let's just quickly recap on what you DO need to have done before you start making more plans.

You should already have…

1. Made a decision about extending your holiday before or after the cruise; your cruise company may have access to good value hotel deals.
2. Booked any flights and airport parking.
3. Considered staying overnight in a port hotel before your cruise, especially if travelling by air.

4. Checked if parking is included with your cruise. Either confirm or book with port.
5. Organised transport for your group and luggage to/from the port/airport/hotel.
6. Checked if visas are required. Will the ship arrange? Or you?
7. Checked that your passport has 6 months validity after the end of the cruise.
8. Checked what vaccinations might be needed and when they should be done.
9. Logged into the Cruise Personaliser and completed advance passenger information.

We talked about finding the 'big ticket, must see' attractions but there will be so much more available everywhere you go, and doing something a bit different is what I am all about at portExplore! For instance, one of my recommendations for Hong Kong is a visit to the Hong Kong Monetary Authority, which may sound mad, but the museum, which has a display of coins and notes used throughout Hong Kong history, is on the 55th floor of a skyscraper with amazing views of the Harbour and the Peak. You can take wonderful pictures from there, especially on a clear day, and its free! You could take a harbour boat trip or see the Big Buddha, but you will feel you've seen much more if you follow a few offbeat suggestions and use local ferries and trams. If you know that this is a once in a lifetime trip then go for the main attractions, but no matter how carefully you plan your itinerary the same ports can often turn up again and again. Think outside the box and consider doing something a bit different!

At this point, to avoid confusion I suggest that you start planning port by port - if you try to work on them all at once your brain starts inventing a completely different place - you know, the French Caribbean island with the English harbour, Columbus' landing spot, and the volcano...!). Start with your most anticipated port and work from there. Note all your ideas in the notebook, put sticky tabs on the edges to divide it up, and put all printouts, maps, and ideas ripped out of magazines in the relevant section of your expanding file.

Start with estimating how brave you think you might feel - I think a good measure of that and of what you can expect to do in any particular port almost has its own maths equation:

$$\frac{\text{Unfamiliarity with Port/Country/Language}}{\text{Time}} = (\text{Distance from ship} + \text{Security advice})$$

It is only a bit of fun obviously, and you can't put actual numbers to it, but the principle should help you think things through. For example, if you have visited the port before, or it is in your own country, or you speak the local language and you've only got three hours free, you should be fine to go off for a bit of sightseeing on your own within a sensible distance. That distance would become less if there were security alerts in the area or if you had no real knowledge about the locality or the language but it could increase a lot if there were no security concerns and you had twelve hours in port. This is particularly relevant when asking for advice about what to see ashore, particularly in specialist cruise groups and advice pages on Facebook. Ships spend differing lengths of time in port so just because MaryAnn from Florida got to the Niagara Falls on her overnight stop in New York, it doesn't mean you can do it in a day! As with all things online you have to be a little wary. The answers you will get are only one person's opinion and unless you are a longtime member of a forum and have started to work out who the 'experts' in the group are, you have no real idea who to take advice from, and actually you have no idea if you like the same things. There is a lot of useful advice and help online from other cruisers, and my suggestion would be to join a few groups and evaluate things a little before you start asking questions.

Online forums, in particular, need to be approached with care. It is best to post simple questions and wait for simple answers. They often have members who have long held grudges against each other, and your simple question about 'tenders ashore on Cunard' or similar can sometimes set off an old rivalry that will completely hijack your post and end up as a discussion as to why you should have booked with P&O instead! It's a shame because a lot of people are genuinely helpful, but the unpleasant ones are really dreadful and are best avoided! Forums seem a bit of a dated platform now anyway and, particularly for your first few cruises, I think you will do better looking for a smaller, friendly and supportive group on Facebook that covers the specific area you are interested in.

CRUISE.co.uk is a large UK based travel agent site with offers, reviews, and a cruising forum that covers everything you could need, plus a lot that you probably don't with discussions in the forum on absolutely everything you could think of (cruise related or not) as well as last-minute offers and Roll Calls. There is a lot of discussion and information on the cruise port discussion pages, but it is never edited or updated so be careful. With regard to train/bus times and services... CHECK! Reviews are written in exchange for a free book or entrance into a competition so they can be of variable standard. If you ever post one, it is best to avoid looking at the comments that people make as they can get pretty unpleasant and personal! They also have a Facebook group which is a good source of last minute cruise deals.

Cruisecritic is probably the bigger UK based travel agent site, and its online forum at https://boards.cruisecritic.co.uk/ is well supported. This site is also one of the main sources of organised excursions that we discuss in Chapter 5, and they publish fairly brief summaries of most cruise ports. Again the forum has its long-term enemies, but this is probably the better site for Roll Calls which seem to attract a truly international group of genuinely helpful members. Within the general forums, of which there are many, you still have to take care to avoid stirring up old rivalries and oneupmanship.

Facebook is where all the cruise lines will have their own official, unofficial, open, closed and possibly 'completely bonkers' pages! To show what I mean, here is a range of pages for Celebrity Cruises (see page 32).

These groups can be quite useful for general cruise information relating to that specific cruise line and life aboard its ships but probably not best for unbiased ideas of what to do ashore. For general questions about life on board, as well as suggestions for things to do in port, you are probably better with more general 'cruise oriented' pages run by online travel agents/travel clubs or free groups with a private discussion space. There are also 'concierge type' subscription membership sites offering location-specific port excursion advice which is almost like having your own personal online travel planner, worth looking for if you want to make life very easy for yourself! Search on Youtube too for videos on ports and cruising and look out for travel/cruise related podcasts. I have listed some of my personal favourite sites which I have used to find out general information and to research different ports in the past. You will definitely be able to find others!

Group	Link	Description
Celebrity Cruises	www.facebook.com/ UKcelebritycruises	Official Celebrity Cruises facebook group.
Celebrity Cruise Line all aboard	www.facebook.com/ groups/715184035190083/?ref=br_ rs	Unofficial Celebrity Cruises page.
Celebrity Cruises Captains Club	https://www.facebook.com/groups/ CelebrityCaptainsClub/?ref=br_rs	Official Celebrity Cruises page for members of their loyalty scheme
The search title is Celebrity Equinox – Grand Cayman Cruise, but the link is actually to Island Marketing Group	https:// grandcaymancruiseexcursions.com/ cruise-ship/celebrity-equinox/ grandcaymancruiseexcursions.com/ cruise-ship/celebrity-equinox/	A business site for a local travel company, which specifically targets Celebrity passengers, calling at their port and looking for a cruise.
#CelebrityCruisesFail	https://www.facebook.com/ groups/236791893529177/about/	Open group dedicated to complaints about Celebrity Cruises
Atlantis March 2019 Cruise - Celebrity Edge	https://www.facebook.com/groups/ march2019atlantisedge/?ref=br_rs	Closed Group for people booking a specific Celebrity Cruise

Group	Link	Description
Cruise Addicts Community Rate, Rant & Review	https://www.facebook.com/groups/176262966119470/?ref=br_rs	Friendly, helpful and supportive free membership. Group covering all aspects of cruising. Also blog
Avid Cruiser	https://www.facebook.com/pg/avidcruiser/posts/?ref=page_internal	Professional general cruise information, port information, tips and news. Also covers river cruises.
portExplore	https://www.facebook.com/profile.php?id=2041977916030587&ref=br_rs	Friendly, helpful and supportive page focusing on discussion about time spent ashore.
Toms ports guides	https://www.facebook.com/TomsPortGuides/	Friendly free extremely detailed port guides with GPS coordinates and lots and lots of detail.
talkExplore	https://www.facebook.com/groups/1532313766817210/?ref=br_rs	Friendly, helpful free membership Group offering port based discussions and advice. Good downloadable port profiles. Also podcast.
Tips for travellers	https://www.facebook.com/TipsForTravellers/	General for all travel advice but cruises are also well covered. Good videos, also lots to find on YouTube.
Little Grey Box	https://www.facebook.com/LittleGreyBox/	Highly personable general travel advice, not cruise related but very informative on relevant destinations. Also on YouTube.
Tours by locals	https://www.toursbylocals.com/	Pricey for two but good for small groups, maybe for a Roll Call group. Very good for ideas of alternative things to do in a city.

Over the time I have been involved in running these types of sites, I have learnt that, as with many things in life, what you get out of these groups directly depends on what you put in. In particular, you will find that the quality of advice received directly depends on the question that was asked! So for this question;

    ❝ Hello. Hop on Hop off buses. What are they like? Regular? Packed? Do you need to prebook? For closer cities to the ports? New to cruising and its taken two years to save up so though we want to enjoy our special holiday all the extras are starting to sound scary. Any tips? (Will do an RC excursion for Rome as a bit of a distance and don't want to be left behind!) Doing the Italian Med nxt June. Gib, Nice, Florence/Pisa, Rome (Civitav.) Naples, Cagliari Sardinia, Seville. Many thanks. ❞

The enquirer got hundreds of replies; they were all answering different sections of the question, but in the main didn't refer to which bit of the question they were in response to. Everyone was trying to be helpful but most of what was received would have been of very little use in planning. In contrast, this question;

    ❝ Hi. Trying to find out the hotel in Civitavecchia. Arriving Rome Fiumicino at 14.30 Saturday & planning stay in Civitavecchia before joining ship Sunday TIA ❞

received this answer –

> ❝ Highly recommend Hotel De La Ville in Civitavecchia. Great value room with fabulous terrace and we've been able to pay a little extra to allow late check out at 5 pm for our late night flight home. Well worth it as I chill out here on the terrace!
> BTW Shuttle from Fiumincino costs about 60€ takes an hour. Train about 20€ and about 2 hours. We took the train. ❞

See? Ask better questions, get better answers!

The FaceBook groups for a specific cruise and date are quite similar to the **roll call** service offered by some cruise discussion forums, such as Cruise Critic. Both are useful, but Roll Call, in particular, can be extremely useful especially if you are a **solo traveller**. The cruise company usually organises a private small drinks party (a 'meet and mingle') for everyone to meet up on the first day or two of the cruise; you should expect at least two senior crew members to attend this. It's worth popping along, especially if you are travelling alone, as it's a great way to get to know people. While some people use the Roll Call or the FaceBook groups just to link up with others who will be aboard and make friends, the best use for them is as an excursion planning tool. A member who is arranging private tours for various ports of call will message it to the group in the hope of finding others who might want to share with them. We will explore this is more detail in the next chapter, but it is definitely worth searching for a Roll Call for your cruise and starting to see what is being discussed for your itinerary. Use your **cruise number** to search for the correct group as a lot of itineraries repeat over a season and a more general search could possibly put you into the wrong group. Even just arranging to share a taxi at one port will make you some new friends and halve the cost.

Don't get so hung up about being on a cruise that you forget that all the usual travel websites and advice pages are still a valuable resource. They won't be of much use for cruise issues, such as where the ship will dock, but you will find lots of recommendations for local tour guides, experiences, and attractions. Again, more in the next chapter, but if you compare **TripAdvisor** with your cruise excursions there will be some quite significant differences. Look at the local **tourist information** office online, especially the 'What's On' section as it may be that your visit coincides with a Festival or Saints Day which could mean that public transport is very crowded or running on a reduced timetable. That might make travel difficult, but why would you plan to go out of town and miss all the local colour of a special festival? It might really be a once in a lifetime experience.

Assuming that there is nothing out of the ordinary happening in town the tourist information sites are still a valuable resource where you can access all sort of useful stuff; they can be absolutely wonderful at responding to email enquiries with pdfs of information leaflets. You can often telephone the office for a conversation, and they will offer to post you maps and guides for the area. Later you will meet people on board who will say "oh, we just pop into tourist information and get a map when we arrive"… but half the ship will be in the same queue, and with a bit of forward planning, you will be ahead of them all.

Guidebooks are always of limited use on a cruise; they often don't even show the port or the dock. Unless you have unlimited luggage allowance, they are probably not worth the hassle although I have known people just cut out the relevant pages and bin the rest of the book! Don't forget that the ship's library will have guidebooks, usually reference only, but if you want to check something while you're on board that could be useful. Mention of books and libraries may seem very low tech, but one of the least anticipated problems that cruisers have on board is dealing with the reduced access to the smartphone led lifestyle that we all take for granted ashore. Internet service aboard is woefully expensive and slow, some of the newer ships have slightly better systems, but the bottom line is that your internet is coming from the same satellite connection that is running the entire ship, its navigation, accounting, bookings, communication – so 3000 people WhatsApping, downloading and 'FaceBooking' would quickly overload the system and the easiest way for the ship to restrict access is to make it extremely expensive. If you are ever offered unrestricted internet as a booking incentive take it, it will be much better value than a free speciality restaurant meal or even a week's free parking! Often people assume that because their phone contract has data included and is valid for the geographical area they are cruising that they will be able to use it onboard. Sadly that isn't true, you can usually get a signal in port with no problem, but it dies off very quickly once you leave port and head offshore. The bottom line is that you can't use tech in the way you would onshore unless you have an unlimited budget, so planning to quickly check out your next destination on Tripadvisor the evening before will waste a lot of your time and money, which is why I suggest you get ahead now!

It's a good idea to check how many other ships will be in port at the same time as you. You can do this at cruisetimetables.com or on whatsinport.com. Search for the country, then the port, and then under 'cruise calendar' you will find a list of the other ships that will be in port that day. The smaller the port, the more important this information is, for example on August 8th 2018 eight cruise ships docked in Santorini over the same day – and that is a lot of people on one cable car! You will be able to see the times the ships are scheduled to arrive and how long they will stay, which will tell you how busy the port will be - extremely as it turns out in this example! These ports are used to handling large groups so it won't be a massive problem and ships tours will all have allocated excursions so if you are booking one of those there is no rush, but if you are planning on hiring a jeep or a private guide to go trekking then you might want to get on and book that before someone else does.

Once you have an idea of what you might want to see or do in each port, then you need to think about how you are going to achieve it. Basically your choices are an **organised excursion**, which you might book through the ship or through a specialist cruise excursion company (in the next chapter we will explain in more detail what the benefits of each are and how you choose which you want to use), or you could use a local **independent guide** who you would book with directly, normally sourced through the sort of online resources I have previously described.

You will get good recommendations and personal introductions if you ask the right question on the right site; it's a good idea to ask how long ago they visited, just in case 'George the amazing taxi driver' retired ten years ago! The third option is to organise a self-guided itinerary for the day yourself, using **local transport options**, car hire, ferries, hop-on-hop-off (HOHO) buses and on foot. Local bus and ferry information will be online; there are often links on the whatsinport.com individual port page, or you can contact the tourist information office. Go to the same places for train timetables or take a look at themaninseat62.com which has information and links for train travel worldwide, or loco2.com which specifically covers Europe. Don't just check journey length, also check frequency (make sure you are checking the right day. If you are there on a Sunday it could be a reduced service) both for the outward and return journey. Many places, especially in Europe, have a slightly dead time in the timetable around the afternoon siesta, particularly on ferry timetables, so make SURE that there will be a train/ferry/bus that will get you back early as well as a backup second option that will also get you back to the port in plenty time before the ship leaves. If you are doing a **DIY** journey, you MUST plan for contingencies and always know what you will do if your first plan falls apart! The ship WILL leave without you if you are not back, even if you are a famous British Member of Parliament who has been booked as a guest speaker, just ask Alan Johnson!

Many ports have **port shuttles** to the nearest town, and you will often find you have a **HOHO bus or boat** option as well. There are two main operators of the

HOHO, City Sightseeing and Big Bus Tours; you can check online for which ports they cover and the routes they take. Although you can buy tickets online, I wouldn't, as you will still have to queue, so you might as well buy them as you board. It would be maddening to have paid for the HOHO bus in advance only to find that the queue for the free port shuttle is shorter! Both companies give discounts if you used them in a previous port (you take your last ticket with you to claim the discount) so maybe check who covers which ports before boarding your first bus! When you are close to a town these buses are a reasonable and reliable way of getting about. They run pretty frequently, provide a map, and run a recorded commentary which can be of variable value. Make sure you ask about the timings of the last bus back to the port and aim for the one before as they get very busy!

Car hire can be a good option if you want to get out of a town and into the surrounding countryside. Islands, in particular, lend themselves to a bit of self-drive, if they're small enough you will always come back to where you started! Price up various options, we have often got brilliant deals on 4x4 jeeps which are fun and once, memorably, had a soft top sports car waiting for us at the bottom of the gangway in Livorno! Always ask for a sat-nav if available. Look to see where the main hirers are in each port; check if they will bring the car to you to save time. See if you can find one company that covers all of the ports that you are considering, it would be worth joining their loyalty scheme and asking for reductions if you are going to hire in more than one location. Also, try to get a reservation package with no cancellation charges in case the ship does not dock; companies that are used to dealing with cruise passengers are usually quite happy to do this. You will need a valid driving licence from your own country and normally an International Driving Permit which you arrange through your local motoring organisation (AAA/AA/RAC/NRMA) for a small fee. If you are hiring within Europe using a UK driving licence, you will also need to have a DVLA check code which replaces the paper licence (they are only valid for 21 days after issue so don't apply too soon). When thinking about a driving route plan to drive to the furthest point of your day then work back. That way you are always driving closer to the ship as the day goes on and you will miss meeting any crowds disembarking from the ship's coach tours, that for some reason almost always work in the opposite direction!

Keep on reading and researching about each individual port until you have a few ideas about what you want to do, keep notes in your notebook under each individual port's own section, print out quotes, and in the next chapter we will move onto who you should organise things through, why that is, and the best time to book them.

CHAPTER 4

WHO TO BOOK WHAT WITH
FINALISING PLANS

Now you have an idea of the sort of thing available in each port you can decide what you want to do. Then we can work out **how** you are going to do it!

It is important to say at this point that if you are travelling with one of the Prestige cruise lines that provide a truly 'all inclusive' service (Silverseas/Regent Seven Seas/Oceania/Viking) they provide some **free excursions** at every port as well as some 'paid-for options' at extra cost. Obviously, if excursions and sightseeing are included in your holiday price then you will probably want to use them. You need to decide which tours you want to do and get on and book them as soon as possible. The most popular will get filled quickly leaving only the 'paid for' or less interesting itineraries to choose from; this is definitely something to remember if you are booking a last-minute cruise with one of these companies. If there is nothing that really appeals then go for a DIY day rather than spending a day seeing something that doesn't float your boat!

Unfortunately for the rest of us free excursions are not the norm; obviously you can arrange a day ashore without spending much if you DIY it, but if you want to be taken somewhere and shown something you will have to pay - the only question really is who are you going to give your money to?

There are three main options for booking your excursions:

1. Through the **cruise line**, either in advance or from the desk onboard ship.
2. Through an **independent cruise excursion** company who will have various offers and package specifically targeting your itinerary.
3. **Privately** with local companies or individual tour guides in each port.

In fact, you will probably want to consider a **combination** of all three methods above as well as a bit of DIY planning but first of all, let's examine all three 'paid for' options before you make any choices and work out the pros and cons of each.

Firstly, let's consider why you might book an excursion with your **cruise company.**

Well for a start they make it **easy** for you! Once you have accessed your cruise personaliser, the tours for each port are ready and waiting for you to download into your own brochure. Advice on the website, as well as the onboard **lectures** and information, will normally focus solely on the sights covered by the tours the ship offers. There will not be much information or advice about any alternatives. Ships Cruise Excursions are expensive, and this will be justified as being because they have individually vetted the providers in each port that will guarantee your satisfaction. In reality, your tour will only be as good as your guide, but there is some truth that these cruise lines (and don't forget the vetting will probably have been done on behalf of the umbrella parent group, i.e. Carnival, whose eight constituent cruise lines will form a large part of each port's visitors) are very important to a port and tour providers will always try to keep the standard high and not upset or disappoint their guests. You are able to pay for excursions using any **onboard credit** (money that may have been allocated to your cabin for you to spend onboard – OBC) that you have from booking incentives or loyalty levels so it may not feel like spending real money! If you intend to use your OBC be careful because if you book excursions up until a couple of weeks before departure your credit card will be charged at the time you book. It's only once you get closer to the cruise that the costs are charged to your ship's account and can be paid with OBC. It's also worth mentioning that if the ship doesn't dock for any reason, there is no argument about getting a **refund** on tour tickets that are cancelled, but if you paid in advance that refund will be made as OBC to your ship's account rather than back to your credit card which can be irritating. Many people feel safer under the **protection of the ship** in the 'bubble' of security around the ship and, because at least one member of the crew accompanies your group in addition to the local guide, it can feel as if you are still in the 'bubble' of the ship's security. Most people will tell you that their main reason for taking a ship's tour is that the **'ship will wait for your return'** whatever the cause of the delay. Unfortunately, this is a bit of a myth and **NOT TRUE!** The ship will always wait for delayed groups if at all possible, but sometimes other factors (see chapter 8) mean that the ship cannot delay its departure. In that case, the cruise company will organise and pay for the cost of everybody to re-join the ship at the next port, which is not quite the same thing, especially if that port is a couple of days away or you have left someone on board! However, this guarantee is an important point in favour of ship's excursions and definitely worth considering if you want to travel a significant distance from the ship. If you want to visit more than one site in a day, you may find that you have to book two 'half day' excursions with a return to the ship in between which is a huge waste of time and money! The groups will use a coach so will be a large group that moves at the pace of the slowest participant. When you add in waiting time for others to shop or take a comfort break it can be a frustrating experience. Tours are graded by level of strenuous activity but just a word about this - there will always be people aboard who are disabled, elderly, or just very slow walkers. They want to go on excursions too so the cruise will always offer one tour labelled 'gentle' or 'level 1' to the biggest attraction at any

TRUE STORY

We arrived at the Peter and Paul fortress to see the tombs of the Czars of Russia. As we got off our minibus with our group of 10, we waved to a table companion who was just arriving in a coach. Our tour guide whisked us to the front of the queue (I suspect with a small bribe) took us in, explained the importance of the site to all Russians and gave us ten minutes to look around. As we left, we met our friend standing with the rest of her group in the entrance queue. We were back in our minibus and away before they had even reached the front of the queue!

port. This helps you gauge how slowly a trip will move or how strenuous a day is really going to be. For example, a mid-range score is probably fine for most people with an ordinary level of fitness and the group will move much faster. Be a little careful of 'strenuous' or level 5 in relation to a sightseeing tour as it normally involves a lot of steps or an uphill walk. In other cases, it is because it is a fast 'rib' or 'banana boat' ride which is only suitable for the really fit and healthy. You will learn to make a decision in relation to your own abilities and fitness levels. In general, I think that anyone who does any regular exercise can probably manage most ships tours unless it is in an extremely hot climate or it involves a lot of jolting around, say in a jeep. Cruise companies are wary of complaints so they will always err on the side of caution; a 'gentle' trip is really very gentle!

BOOK IT? Book beforehand if you want to ensure your place on a particular tour. You will pay when you book and will be refunded to your onboard account if the ship fails to dock. If you can wait until you are aboard then you can pay with OBC.

TOP TIP

Just be careful to check that you actually need to book a tour to visit an attraction at all. For example in Ketchikan, Alaska the local Lumberjack Show is a very popular attraction. Tickets on the door are always available and cost $23. The cruise tour walks you there from the ship in an escorted group; it is just three blocks from the port gate to the show, they charge $45...

Your second option is an **independent cruise excursion** company. There are a few of these in the UK; the most common are Cruising Excursions and Viator, and elsewhere, especially the USA Triptelligent and ShoreTrips are popular, and they are starting to make an impact on the cruising market. You will find *Cruising Excursions,* who are part of Cruise.co.uk, offer packages tailored to your ships itinerary (these even show up as an optional part of your booking on some travel sites, for example, Cruise Nation). The main advantage is that prices are significantly lower than for comparable trips offered by the ship and their USP (at least for now) is that they offer a package deal where prices drop if you bundle together 3,4,5 or even all the excursions on your cruise. The ships don't offer any reductions based on what you book, but I imagine that if they lose custom that will change.

Independent cruise excursion companies offer a slightly extended tour range; there is always a location that doesn't seem to be in the personaliser, either as a stand-alone option or as an addition to a popular trip. Check what is included as I have heard that meals and entrance tickets are not always included and once those costs are added the price may be the same or even more than the ship's price. Trips are similarly graded by how strenuous they are and group sizes are much the same as the ship's tours, normally a full coach, so in the same way large groups will go at the pace of the slowest and have to wait for others to shop or take a comfort break. Where private tours or transfers are offered, they seem expensive, but in all cases, they offer guarantees about getting you back to port (I would try and find out exactly what that means) and a full refund if your ship does not dock for any reason.

These specialist companies deal internationally with excursions and will have as much interest in protecting their reputation and driving a hard bargain with providers as the cruise lines. I suspect that often the excursions for both options come from the same local company. The question is who will get priority for the better vehicles or guides, and the answer is probably whoever is paying (and therefore charging) the most! At this point, I have to declare myself not totally unbiased! We used *Cruising Excursions* from Laem Chabang, Thailand to visit the Grand Palace in Bangkok in early 2018 and were extremely late returning to the ship due entirely to the way the guide had run the day. To be fair, a lot of the people in our group had used the company for all their excursions and had nothing but praise as a whole. Those of us who only met their guide in Thailand had a different view! Again, to be fair Cruising Excursions responded swiftly to our letter of complaint with a full refund and the result of their investigation, the upshot being that our guide no longer had a job! We haven't yet used CE again, but they are so much cheaper and have a wider offering that we just might...

BOOK IT? Booking beforehand is better than waiting until you are on board as you will be able to print tickets and confirmations more easily. Make sure there are full refunds in the event of port cancellations, and try to get a definitive answer as to what would happen if the tour made you miss the ship.

Your third option is to book an excursion with a **private guide or company** sourced independently by you. This takes more planning than either of the other options, but it will give you more control. It almost always

costs less and covers more than the larger group ship's tours. A private guide will usually take individuals or small groups around either on foot or by car in which case their quote should include the cost of the car and driver. They can take you to the main sights, but should be able to tailor the tour to your specific interests. For example, if you want to know more about a local artist, sportsman, or musician then advising your guide when booking will get you a more bespoke themed tour with greater flexibility built into the day. I would avoid using a straightforward Google search to source an individual guide, as you will not be able to evaluate how good or reliable they are. Private guides are best found through personal recommendation by fellow cruisers either in person or in forums, FaceBook groups, Trip advisor, toursbylocals.com or local tourist information offices; I suggest you choose one with some form of accreditation from the local tour guide association. You will find **online reviews** specific to the company or guide so you can see exactly what you will get, and you will be able to have a conversation about exactly what you would like to do by email or phone before booking. Similarly, it is best to do some homework in advance and book a guide rather than relying on finding someone when you arrive; negotiating a price on the dockside gives you no chance to ensure that someone is reputable and trustworthy. A small group of local tour operators may cover more than one port on your itinerary and offer discounts for more than one tour, for example, ALLA tours will cover most of the Baltic ports on your cruise. A big advantage is that because your group size will be significantly smaller than a coach-based group you will move faster, **see more** and spend less time waiting for others. You will often have a local expert guide and **more time** to ask questions, and tours can be more specialised and targeted. Depending on the size of the group, there may be an opportunity to discuss any **alterations** to the itinerary you would like to make, but beware that in many cultures the practically obligatory 'shopping' stop is almost impossible to get rid of without causing offence. We have found it simplest to say we don't want to go and then to show no interest if it still happens; that way you are quickly on your way again! Quite often someone will organise a private tour for a particular port and then use **roll call** to find others to share it with them. You could do this yourself if you like, it's a good way to get exactly what you want, meet other passengers, and reduce costs. In the main, guides dealing with the cruise industry understand that on occasion a ship will be unable to dock, and they rarely seem to ask for payment in advance, however if you are taking responsibility through roll call and you are asked to pay in advance, you will need to be sure that your insurance will cover cancellations. Some people ask for money up front from people who have agreed to share, but others don't, it is your call. Roll Call is particularly useful to investigate if you are travelling solo as it gives you a good way to meet people online before you actually join the ship. It also helps you plan alternatives to organised excursions without the safety concerns that you might have travelling alone.

Most local tour guides and companies will mention a 'back to the ship' guarantee and promise that you will be back on board in good time and they obviously have good local support and the knowledge to back that up, however they may not have the resources to be able to promise to get you to the next port if things go wrong.

BOOK IT? As always, beforehand is better than waiting until you are on board, as it is easier to make enquiries, print tickets etc. Make sure your insurance covers port cancellation if you are paying money in advance.

Your fourth option is **self-guided exploring**. You can decide where you want to go and what you want to see; this might include fewer museums and more sitting in market squares and people watching, or it might be a frantic dash around to see every Bellini statue in Venice. You could use local transport, or hire a car and go inland to the mountains, or just take a taxi to a beach. A self-guided day gives you a chance to see one thing in great detail, better opportunities to take photos without waiting for fifty other people to take one too, and the chance to look for the heart of a city rather than its monuments. I do find it odd that people can get a little programmed and forget to be an individual when they are on a cruise, taking tours that cram in as many sights and attractions as possible.

TOP TIP

Don't feel pressured into visiting the sights at all if you fancy a day on the beach! No one has the right to judge your choices, and there is no such thing as a waste of a day if you have spent it doing what YOU want to do. It is your cruise not anyone else's. Have fun!

If you want to go to dinner knowing that you will have been to all the same places as your table companions, a self-guided day is not for you! Obviously going it alone is not practicable or sensible everywhere, for example in Russia it is actively discouraged, and the cost of an individual visa can be more than the cost of a two-day tour with included group visa.

Self-guided exploring is usually our first choice as we are just not 'coach trip, waiting in line' sort of people, and to be honest we would almost always prefer to do something away from the guided excursions and crowds even if it means we get nowhere near the 'for' destination! We prefer to get off the ship under our own steam and use local transport, HOHO buses, car hire, or even just walk. We don't feel pressured to see anything in particular or try to pack too much in. It is meant to be a holiday after all, and we really don't like to cut it fine. I always aim to be safely back on board at least an hour before the ship sails!

Research is key to a successful day ashore under your own steam, especially in separating yourself from everyone else disembarking at the same time and getting away quickly. We book anything we can ahead to avoid time spent waiting in queues especially train or ferry tickets and also entrance tickets for anything we want to visit. If you book car hire ahead, they will often deliver it to the dockside for you. This is where the overall arc of the cruise is important in planning what you want to do. The sort of thing you want to think about is how tired you will be. Never plan a complicated self-guided day or hire a car for a long drive inland on the first day of a cruise if you know you will be jet-lagged or tired. You need to be alert when you are on your own. Also, how unfamiliar are you with the country, language or alphabet? It's difficult to be independent if you can't even read the signs! How in need of exercise do you think you will be? After a long flight or a couple of sea days, you might just want to get off the ship and take a bike ride or walk, not sit on a coach all day.

Self-guiding doesn't mean always shunning ships tours and heading off on your own. Actually, if we wanted to visit somewhere a couple of hours or more from the ship we quite often use the "on your own' ships' tour option; this is basically just the cruise company providing a coach to get you to the main tourist attraction but leaving you free to explore on your own once there. Even if it we know it would be cheaper to use the local train, we do like the advantage that once you rejoin the group at the end of the day you are under the 'back to the ship' guarantee, especially useful if there are delays en route or if the next port is an airline flight away.

We use local tour companies too especially if we want to visit more than one site in a day. For example at our Piraeus stop we know that we can get to the Acropolis easily by public transport and we could use a local guide once there, but if we also wanted to add in a trip to see the Corinth Canal which is an hour outside Athens then we would use a private tour, squeeze every last moment from the day and trust them to get us back on board. We find self-guided visits more relaxing and enjoyable; they make us feel that we've really visited a city, not just been shown it through a glass bubble.

BOOK IT? Well 'plan it' anyway! Just be aware that any tickets bought in advance may not be covered unless you have 'missed port' insurance although this is not really a problem, just worth bearing in mind for 'tender' ports.

SO TO SUM UP...

A **ship's tour** is the best option for you if:

- You are the slightest bit nervous about being in an unfamiliar place.
- You are concerned about security or health issues.
- You want to travel far from the port.
- You want to pay for cruises using onboard credit from loyalty or booking credit.
- The excursions are included in the cost of your cruise.

An **independent cruise excursion** tour is the best option for you if:

- You want to save money – just be sure of what you will pay extra for on the day.
- You want to book a package for the whole cruise.
- You are the slightest bit nervous about being in an unfamiliar place.
- You want to travel far from port and squeeze as much sightseeing as possible into the day.

A **private tour** is the best option for you if:

- You hate the slow pace and 'one size fits all' feel of large group excursions by coach.
- You are looking for value for money.

- You want to visit more than one attraction without returning to the ship in between.
- You are not confident enough in a country or language to completely go it alone.
- You have a specialist interest that a large group tour won't cover.
- You want to meet up with others on board.

A **DIY day** is the best option for you if:

- You are a fairly confident person, happy to explore a strange city without a guide.
- You have visited that port before and want to do something different this time.
- You are in a port where you can walk off the ship and straight into town.
- You just want a quiet day without being shown things and herded around.
- You are happy to research a travel plan and plan exactly where to go and what to see.
- You are a portExplorer!

CHAPTER 5

GETTING READY TO GO
WHAT YOU WILL NEED WITH YOU

About six weeks before your cruise you need to start your **final checks**. This is when you need to make sure that nothing has changed and to confirm arrangements, some of which will have been put in place months ago. It is the time to think things through from the beginning and make sure nothing has got missed or muddled.

Firstly check for up to date security and visa information for all the countries you will be visiting. In the UK this would be through the Foreign Office www.gov. uk/foreign-travel-advice and in the USA The Department of State https://travel.state.gov. It is important that you check the advice that your own country gives as it will vary. Knowing that you wouldn't need a visa if you were English will not help you get through Immigration if you are Mexican! You may not need an individual visa, as it is often organised as a **whole ship visa** through the cruise line, but check for changes and take advice if necessary. I cannot stress how important it is to check that things have not changed – we once booked a cruise more than a year ahead and did not need to have a visa at that point, when we arrived at the airport it turned out that now we did...

Secondly, check up to date health and vaccination advice hasn't changed. In the USA that is through the same State Department website, in the UK through the

National Travel Health Network https://nathnac.net/. Again make sure you are checking the site for the country you live in (if in doubt contact the cruise line for advice). Make sure you have any vaccination certificates you will need and put them in your folder ready to go.

Thirdly, find your passport. I have mentioned before that you need to have six months validity after your return date but if for some reason this has been missed you now have six weeks to renew it. If you can't find it, you have six weeks to get a new one!

Your passport will also be needed for the mountain of photocopying or scanning that you are about to begin. It is best to make a complete set of your documents to take with you – packed separately from your original documents, a second set to leave home in case of emergency (make sure you have told someone where to find them!) and, for real peace of mind I usually email myself a set as well.

I would include the following documents as required:

1. Passport.
2. Visas.
3. Child travel consent form – permission from any parent who is not travelling with you, specifically if you have a different surname from the child.
4. Cruise confirmation, itinerary and contact details.
5. Hotel confirmations and contact details.
6. Travel insurance details.
7. Flight or other tickets.
8. Doctors prescription for any prescription drugs you will be taking with you.

9. Driving licence/International Driving Permit/DVLA certificate.
10. Emergency contact phone list with international codes.
11. List of credit cards and international numbers to call for customer assistance.

About a month before you go it is best to go back to your notebook and envelopes for each port, review all your plans – check for any gaps in your plans and fill in or leave free for a bit of spontaneity! It is a good idea to send emails to **confirm** that everything you previously booked is in place, ask for local contact numbers in case of emergency, and also for confirmation of an exact meeting place. Make sure you have all the relevant receipts and documents to hand, either printed out or downloaded and accessible on your phone. If you need cash to pay guides or hire companies on arrival, then you can add that to your individual port envelopes in the relevant currency when you have it to hand.

Cruises usually have their own challenges in terms of local **currency**. You may be lucky and only need to use one throughout the entire cruise, but it is more common to need at least two or three different ones. It is worth taking the time to work out what currency and credit cards you want to take with you. For your cards, the general advice is to let your bank or **credit card provider** know that you will be travelling so that your card is not suddenly declined if an overseas transaction is made. In reality, some companies seem grateful that you have rung, and others say it is not necessary to tell them, but it is probably better to be safe than sorry and advise them so that you know your card will not be declined in error. If you are travelling to **Cuba** you will need a card that has **not** been issued by an American bank or company which can be difficult; also you cannot exchange American dollars there for local money (interestingly the best currency to take to Cuba is the Canadian dollar). Cruises can be quite complicated in terms of different currencies for different ports especially when the local currency is 'closed' and not able to be bought or sold abroad. You might want to note the local currencies and which ones you will need into your checklist/notebook, especially if you will need cash to put into your envelopes to pay tour guides, possibly even add it to your itinerary to help keep track.

Using our example (page 60), you can see how this is helpful to get your thoughts in order, as although we are visiting six countries, we will only need four different currencies. We also see the most commonly advised currency for local use or exchange is the US$. We can make an estimate of how much we are likely to need in each port and then take some emergency cash in dollars. The onboard account is also in dollars so we can use them to pay our stateroom account if we have any left over which will save transaction charges.

An alternative to planning and juggling various currencies is a pre-paid currency card such as Monzo, Travelex or Revolut. You transfer money to your card account via an app; the card then functions as a normal debit card would, but it makes payments in any local currency without any currency or transaction charges. It works best if you are travelling to urban destinations which

Date	Port	Currency	Available?	Best rate or alternative	Estimate of money needed £ ££ £££
S11	Civitavecchia, Rome, Italy	Euro	Y	US$	Local travel/ coffee breakfast £
M12	Catania, Sicily Italy	Euro	Y	US$	3-hour tour and back to ship. Pay cash locally £
W14	Piraeus, Athens, Greece	Euro	Y	US$	Whole day ashore public transport lunch entrance fees ££
S17	Aqaba, Jordan	Jordanian Dinar	Y	US$	Tour booked & paid inc lunch. Drinks, souvenirs & tips only £
F23	Muscat Oman	Omani Rial	Y	GB£	Tour booked on Roll call- need 35OR cash Drinks, souvenirs & tips only £
S24	Abu Dhabi UAE	UAE Dirham	Y	US$	Evening tour??
S25	Abu Dhabi UAE	UAE Dirham	Y	US$	Grand Prix day out £££££ !
M26	transfer to Dubai	UAE Dirham	Y	US$	Whole day ashore late flight £££

are used to accepting card transactions for most things, that way you can use it as a debit card and pay for small things such as a coffee or a bus ticket just as you would at home, and in other parts of the world you can use it at an ATM to get cash, as this is usually preferable to a card transaction and will sometimes get you a better price. A combination of cash, backup currency, currency/debit card, and credit card will give you the fullest range of options. I am so bad with numbers, especially when there are more than a couple of noughts on the end, that I usually prepare a **currency cheat sheet**. That way I don't end up buying something on a credit card that is much more expensive than I expected! If you are good with numbers then you don't need to don't bother, but I find the 10-fold differences that you get between currencies, especially in Asia, extremely difficult. Just looking at the chart above I know I would be particularly confused between Oman and the UAE and start worrying that we had just got in the most expensive taxi in the world!! I could use a currency conversion app, but a bit of paper folded in my wallet with the money works well for me and is more instant, especially if you have a low or non-existent signal.

£	Euro	US$	Jordinian Dinar	Omani Rial	UAE Dirham
1	1.12	1.30	0.92	0.5	4.79
10	11	13	9	5	48
100	112	130	92	50	479
1000	1123	1304	9245	502	4787
10000	11225	13029	9249	5017	47864

I have to admit that as much as I love my **smartphone** at home, I often find it of limited use on cruises. The combination of different countries and the onshore/offshore complications with call charges mean that you have to be really careful to avoid receiving a very large bill! On the other hand, it is one of the things that makes cruising so special; it is not often that you can be completely unreachable for a couple of days! Calls are difficult when at sea, and things get even more complicated when you add data to the picture, so first of all let's sort out the call/text/answerphone issue.

The first thing to consider is where you are and where your phone thinks that it is! EU legislation has removed roaming charges within the EU; all phone contracts include service in any other member country at no extra charge. That includes places which, although officially in the EU, are geographically well outside it - such as the Azores, Canary Islands, Madeira, Guadeloupe, French Guiana, Martinique, and Reunion. But other countries that are geographically 'in' Europe such as Albania and Bosnia are not free (even though Croatia which is between them is included!). Similarly, some American providers include calls from Canada and Mexico in your contract cover, but others don't. Your phone provider will have details of which countries they cover, and they usually list them in **different package** levels. These groups differentiate between where your contract minutes and data are available to use at no extra charge (as in Europe, above) or where they can be used for a daily flat rate charge. There may be different groupings with different prices according to the countries geographical location in the world. The most far-flung or inaccessible places will usually not be included in a package but only available on a pay **by the minute** option.

Cruises have their own challenges as you could quite easily be cruising between countries in different groups, for example, a Caribbean cruise could take in two islands 'in Europe' - where calls might be free as above, one that is in the 'World Traveller' level such as Jamaica - where calls and data are included in a daily rate and another such as Cuba where you are charged by the minute to make or receive a call, and there is no data service available.

The situation gets even more complicated as you travel between ports because the ships communication system will quickly override a weak signal from the shore, and your phone will connect to a very expensive **at-sea** provider, such as Cellular At Sea or Wireless Maritime Services. These are considered to be out of 'out of contract' roaming and charges which are made by the minute to make or receive a call are extremely high. Texting would cost significantly less, but our best advice is to consider turning your phone to Airplane Mode as soon as you get onboard and unless you are certain of the data charges in a port you should turn off data roaming ashore in order to avoid a huge bill!

To sum up:

- It isn't where you actually are in the world that matters but which roaming package the country is allocated. Those country groupings will change between different providers.
- Always call your provider for advice, be **specific** about the places you are visiting.

- Even if your cruise takes place wholly within your contract country or area, calls made at sea will **not** be included.
- If your phone is switched on and it connects to places that have a different contract grouping you will be charged that daily rate just to receive the welcome text. This can happen a lot in the Caribbean as you pass close to other islands. Putting your phone on Airplane mode reduces the chance of an unexpected bill.

Any data that is included in your phone contract is treated in the same way as call charges; it will vary from country to country. Don't forget that where you are able to access data at all speeds may be quite slow. Many parts of the world now expect 4G as standard but in other places 3G is the norm and quite often it is only available in limited areas within a country.

On board your best option would be to sign up for an internet package, the ship's connection will almost certainly be quite slow and clunky, but it will be better than nothing. The newer ships are trying to improve internet access and speed, but it is never as good as at home. It can be very expensive too. Free minutes are often given as a perk for different loyalty levels or cabin grades. Occasionally you can get a special offer when you buy a 'whole cruise' or a 'by the minute' package in the first few days of the cruise. Do a little homework before you go, be certain which ports you can use your phone normally in and which you will need to find free Wi-Fi. That will help you decide what level of internet access you want to sign up for onboard.

There are quite a few **travel apps** that are useful when travelling, some of them are targeted directly at cruisers and some provided by individual cruise lines. I would definitely do a bit of investigation and download any that you think you will want to use before you leave home, as downloading an app over the ship's Wi-Fi is slow and expensive! Quite a lot of cruise lines are starting to improve their communications offering onboard, and many now have their own app which sometimes includes an instant messaging service that you can use whilst at sea. You will find the most up to date information about this in your Cruise Personaliser, but if there is an app for your cruise, then I would definitely encourage all of your group to download it. Other apps that I would consider are the Berlitz phrasebook and translator, and the Shipmate app (for its cruise countdown if nothing else!). Search for local travel apps; most cities now have a system that helps you in real time, using your location to give information about buses, trams, or metros nearby. These are definitely worth using but don't forget that the things you use day to day such as Google maps, Google translate, Foursquare, Uber, and even Pokémon GO will work in most countries if you have the data available to use them!

As we have already mentioned, conventional guidebooks are of limited use. You could download digital guidebooks as you need them (DK, Lonely Planet, and Rough Guides all do them, check if they will be useful for your itinerary), download and print cruise related port guides for your individual ports or even cannibalise your guidebooks and just take the pages and maps that you need. You will always be able to get a basic map of the port from Guest Services, and there is normally a tourist office handing them out once you are ashore; obviously it will save you time queuing if you managed to get someone to post you a map when you were doing your planning!

I am not going to cover 'packing for a cruise' in this book as such, but I did want to make a few suggestions about things that it might be useful to take with you dependant on where you are going:

- A **bag** that you can use to take out for a day ashore;this might be a backpack or a beach bag. People quite often travel to the ship with a small cabin bag as hand baggage and then realise that they don't really have a bag suitable to take to the beach. You will normally find a complimentary cruise company bag in your cabin, but I would always avoid using anything that marks you out as coming from the ship, not least because prices will rocket as soon as a shopkeeper sees it!

- For the same reason, I would consider taking a couple of **beach towels** if you are intending to go to the beach. I sat on a beach in Thailand and watched as a Thai Massage lady spoke to every person on the beach with a blue and white striped 'Princess' towel – if you want to be left alone, take your own. If they were cheap enough, you could always leave them behind and free up luggage space/weight for your homeward journey.

- Staying with beach days don't forget a **waterproof case** that you can slip money and credit/cabin cards into so that you don't need a 'bag monitor' to stay on shore.

- If you have your own **snorkelling gear,** I would take your own snorkel and mask (especially if it is to prescription) which will always be nicer than anything you hire.

- Also **beach shoes** for climbing around on rocks, you don't want to waste time trying to buy them when you get there, especially for kids.
- A mini travel **first aid kit** that contains enough to get you patched up and back to the ship rather than potentially having to visit a clinic or hospital.
- Insect repellent, sunscreen, hat. I know you can get these locally, but why waste time?
- Other destinations may suddenly be much colder than you expect, we met snow in Bergen in May! A pull-on **hat and gloves** at the bottom of your backpack are useful. If you expect it to be cold take portable gel **hand warmers** and a **space blanket**.
- A disposable **poncho** or an **umbrella** may well come in useful pretty much anywhere!
- A small supply of **boiled sweets** are useful for travel nausea.
- A **power pack** to charge your mobile phone and spare **batteries** for your camera.
- ALL the correct **chargers,** plugs and leads!
- A backpack that doubles as a **camera bag** is less noticeable to others than a conventional camera bag.
- A different **SD card** for every port means less chance of losing all your pictures or otherwise upload them daily.
- Pocket **tissues** and hand sanitiser.
- A **torch**, no reason, but always useful!
- Some **cereal bars** (or similar) are useful to take ashore as emergency snacks. Don't rely on taking fruit from breakfast as many countries do not allow you to take fruit ashore from a cruise ship.

- I always love to have a couple of novels on holiday that are set in the area I am visiting, ask at your local bookshop or try www.tripfiction.com for ideas.

This is obviously not an exhaustive list! You need to think about your plans for each day and visualise what you are going to do and think about what you might need. It is one of the challenges of cruising that you can be on a beach holiday one day, trekking a jungle path the next, and sightseeing in a large city on the third. It really can be like planning for different holidays that all run at the same time!

CHAPTER 6

GOING ASHORE
YOUR ARRIVAL AND DAY IN PORT

It's time to get organised for your day ashore and you should begin your preparations the **evening before** arriving in port. Firstly, pop down to **guest services** and ask for the most up to date information about the next day's port of call. They should know if there are any **planned alterations** to the expected time of arrival or departure, and also be aware of any predicted weather conditions that might cause a problem. They should also be able to give you a simple **map of the port** and mark on it where the ship is likely to dock or where the **tender** will arrive ashore. If the ship is docking **alongside**, they should know how many **gangways** will be in use and what decks they are likely to be on. This might give you a head start in the morning; usually they are quite low down in the ship, often somewhere near the Medical Centre, but it can vary with the port and the tide. The side that the gangway will be situated on will be dictated by the way the ship docks – once the ship has stopped it will be pretty obvious!

If you are booked onto a **ship's tour**, you should already have your tickets and your instructions for where and when to meet the group (these are usually delivered in an envelope to the post slot by your cabin door, but occasionally a steward will have laid them on the bed for you, and that is when they often get misplaced!). If you don't have them visit the **shore excursions desk** now to track them down, it will be too late in the morning!

Back in your cabin, check the **daily schedule** sheet for the next day which will have been left in your cabin in the early evening. It is worth packing this to take ashore with you the next day (or photographing the relevant information to keep on your phone) as it contains six really important pieces of information:

1. **The time that you are expected back to the ship.** This will be clearly marked, normally as 'All Aboard'. This is the time you MUST return by as the ship will be leaving shortly afterwards. If the time has changed from what you expected it is safe to assume that this is the most up to date information. (Always check when you leave the ship anyway, the 'all aboard' time is always displayed at the gangway.).

2. **Information about leaving the ship** – especially if disembarkation is by tender there will be information on how this will be organised. You particularly need to know if they are going to allocate timed tender tickets, as that means you will have to allow time to queue for both the tender tickets themselves and then for access to your allocated tender journey. There will also be information about meeting points, waiting areas, and disability access in the schedule.

3. **Ships time v local time** – this can get confusing. Obviously, it is great when the ship runs to the same time zone as the port, but sometimes it is easier for the ship to stay on the time zone of the previous port. If they are different, you need to be very clear

which time you are working to – if the ship is leaving at 17.00 this is SHIP'S TIME. A watch set to ship's time is easier to rely on than a smartphone that might automatically update to local time.

4. **The contact details of the ship's port agent**. This changes at every port and is VII (Very Important Information). The Port Agent is responsible for anything to do with the ship whilst it is docked and is the person who would have to help you arrange your onward travel if you missed the ship. They are a useful resource if something goes wrong and you are having problems contacting or getting back to the ship.

5. **Information about immigration arrangements**. If you need your passports to go ashore, they will be delivered to you in your cabin. Normally this doesn't happen, your Cruise card effectively acts as your passport, and the ship holds your passport and carries out all immigration paperwork whilst you are ashore. You will still get the relevant immigration stamps in your passport, but this system saves time. If it is necessary for you to have your passport in a particular country, then you will have it. Information for local Embassies and Consulates is often printed in the Daily Schedule in case of emergency. If there is a daily 'port charge' from the local authorities, it will be mentioned in the bulletin; this will not an be an optional charge, the ship is charged it on a per head basis. Whether you go ashore or not it will be on still be on your stateroom account.

6. **Shuttle buses information**. If you are arriving at a large commercial port, then you will not be allowed to walk freely around it. The cruise line will run a shuttle bus to the nearest town. This may be free, or you may be charged for it, sometimes the difference is due to cabin type or the type of fare booked for the cruise (saver fares often exclude free shuttles, and you have to purchase a ticket that others get free). If you will have to pay, check before boarding that the Port Authority isn't also running a free bus to the Dock Gate.

It is worth taking some time to get together the essentials for the next day. Take a look at my **daily disembarkation checklist** below. It may all seem fairly obvious, but it is important, and we learnt some of it from bitter experience! Other things you may want to take include: water, camera, snacks, sunglasses, sunscreen, towels, binoculars, rain jackets, hat, snorkels – it all depends on the plans you have made so I will leave that up to you!

Finally, you might want to consider booking a room service breakfast for the morning; this will mean you can avoid the crowds and just leave your cabin ready to go ashore. (This option is not available on the last day of your cruise.)

On the **morning of arrival**, it is worth getting up early to watch the ship come in, this is particularly true in picturesque places such as Kotor and Venice but even when it is not a particularly beautiful approach this will help you **get your bearings** and see where the ship is docking in relation to the town or other landmarks. Once the ship

DAILY DISEMBARKATION CHECKLIST

CRUISE CARD: You need to show this to leave the ship. Without it, you will not be allowed off, and you will have to go back to your cabin and collect it! PLEASE do not forget it!

PORT AGENT CONTACT DETAILS: Take the daily schedule with you or a photo on your phone.

PASSPORT COPY/ ID: Photocopy of your passport or photo on your phone. ID useful to claim any age-related, student or professional discounts, whilst ashore and purchasing age-restricted items.

PHONE: Even if you do not intend to use your phone ashore it is best to have it with you just in case of emergency.

PHONE CHARGER: Take an emergency power pack. If things go wrong at the end of the day and your phone is already low on charge, you will need it to keep in touch with the ship. At the very least take the charger lead.

DRIVING LICENCE: plus International Driving Permit or DVLA check code as needed.

MONEY & CREDIT CARD: Obviously, you need some money when you go ashore but take a credit card with you as a backup, just in case!

INSURANCE DETAILS: Take the contact details for your travel insurance maybe as a photo on your phone.

MEDICATION: If you take important medication regularly, plan to carry a small amount ashore with you. Lack of access to essential medication could make a bad situation worse. Always carry your current medication list if you are taking tablets ashore, to prove that they are prescribed for you.

BOOKING CONFIRMATIONS: Confirmations, instructions, contact details, portExplore cheatsheet, maps and guidebooks for the day's exciting adventure!

docks it is often another half an hour or so before the ship's completes its arrangements and passengers are allowed to disembark. The captain will make an **announcement** when the gangway is set up. Bear in mind that on a port morning everything will be much busier than on a sea day as pretty much everyone will want breakfast at once (except those who had room service!). If you are on a ship's tour, you will have an allocated meeting area and time. Passengers who have booked private tours and have full days planned will often start queuing on the stairs as soon as the ship is alongside. Quite honestly, if you're not on a very tight schedule, it is best to avoid all that. Go and have a large breakfast in the main dining room (the buffet will be extremely full with added backpacks!) which will mean you don't have to spend time eating a big lunch later! Let everything die down a bit before you go to disembark, if you can, as it can all get a bit busy and some people can get a bit grumpy and stressed. It is a holiday after all, and you are meant to be having fun, so stay out of it all as much as possible, be cheerful and friendly and get off as quickly as you can! **Disregard this advice if you have a specific meeting time arranged!**

If you want to do the opposite, get a head start and get off the ship quickly, you need to be up and about. **Talk to the crew**. Find out what the procedures will be in this port, are there are going to be two **gangways** (one for organised tours and the other for crew/ self-guided passengers)? Ask where these will be, especially on which stairway and deck. If you want to be amongst the first off the ship, you may need to head towards the location of the gangway and start queuing. If it is a tender port, you will definitely need to queue for an early **tender ticket**. You don't need to be ready to leave when you queue for tickets as if you ask nicely you can book seats for a convenient tender later on in the morning. Cruise run excursions will have normally taken priority on the first few tenders, which can be a bit irritating, but the sooner you get to the desk the sooner you will get off the boat.

Water is always available to buy as you exit the ship; there is normally a table with bar staff close to the security desk. If you have an all-inclusive drinks package, it will be worth grabbing a couple of bottles so that you don't have to pay for them ashore. It is worth knowing that while you can take a coffee with you if you are walking off the ship, you are **not allowed** onto a tender with hot drinks.

SLIGHTLY SNEAKY TIP

Most people walk down the stairs to reach the gangway, that's certainly the way you will be directed, and a queue quickly builds up on the stairs. If you arrive at the deck level of the gangway by lift, you might have a bit of smiling and apologising to do, but you can usually get off the ship a bit quicker. It might be worth a try especially if things are very busy...

When you get to the security desk at the top of the gangway you will need to show your **cruise card** to one of the staff on duty who will scan its barcode (there are actually two exit points at security - the left-hand queue always seems to move faster!) You will hear the scanner beep and then they will check the photo of you that pops up on their screen (sometimes they ask you to remove your sunglasses or hat for full identification), this is how the ship can be certain of exactly who is ashore. You are then free to go down the gangway or onto the tender, and to the shore.

Once you are ashore, what you will find varies greatly but if you were up early enough to watch the ship dock you shouldn't get a big surprise! It might be a full-blown airport style **immigration** desk, which might take a long time to pass through in a city like New York or St. Petersburg, or you may be able to just wander off through an open gate and straight out of the port. Usually, there is a reasonable level of security for people coming into the port in order to keep the ship secure, but mainly port staff aren't interested and don't want to see any form of ID when you are leaving, particularly if your previous port was in the same country or economic zone. If you are at a port that also acts as the starting point for cruises or large ferries, then there will always be some sort of port **terminal building**. This will contain anything from some very basic facilities to full-blown 'airport' style terminal with shopping malls, duty-free, and restaurants. There may be tour company and car hire desks, also an official Taxi rank, often with fixed prices. If you have booked a driver or private tour group, they should be waiting for you in this area. (The ship's tour groups will have met onboard and been escorted off together.)

If you see some off-duty crew members sitting around and glued to their phones, you will know that there's a **free WiFi** Hotspot. The internet is so expensive on ships that the crew are real experts in finding it for free when they are ashore.

TOP TIP

Talking to your waiter or cabin steward about an individual port is not a bad idea as they will have probably been there many times before. As well as knowing where to find free WiFi they will probably also know where to find the nearest supermarket or pharmacy. If you've got something you particularly want to buy or do, it is worth having a chat to some of the staff while you are on board; the Entertainment crew always seem to be particularly knowledgeable about local beaches and bars! Once you are off the ship though, it is fairer to leave them alone to enjoy their well-earned leisure time.

In a **transit port**, (a small port that only ever deals with ships that are arriving and leaving on the same day and no joining passengers) you usually walk straight out of the gates into a busy and chaotic scene that can seem quite intimidating. Some people find that this can be really rather unpleasant and feel that they are surrounded by people who want to take them for a ride, literally and possibly metaphorically. If you've already made your plans and are expecting a hire car, driver, or private cruise tour then obviously you can just walk through it all and wave them all away smilingly as you walk to your prearranged meeting point.

If you are picking up a hire car always check before you drive off that you can make the sat-nav talk to you in English (ask for a printed map as backup in case it doesn't work due to poor reception), ask to be shown the location of the spare tyre and locking nuts, and also for a local emergency phone number in case you need help of any kind. Make sure you know where to deliver the car back and what you are expected to do about replacing fuel.

If your plan is to **get a taxi**, then take sensible precautions. Know where you want to go and ask at least two drivers to give you an idea of cost, just to make sure you're not being ripped off. In smaller places there tends to be a pretty fixed price but if you don't ask you won't know! Ask if that price includes a **return pickup** and also if that is on the meter or a fixed price. If you want the driver to come back and pick you up later, then do not pay them in full when they drop you off! If you feel threatened, harassed, or hassled walk away.

TOP TIP

As a general rule you should drive to the furthest point of your itinerary and work your way back towards the port - this gives you a shorter journey back if time is tight or you encounter delays.

In many places, especially in the Caribbean, you can find shared minibuses that charge per person to go to various points around the island, and they can be quite a fun way of getting about. If you have made a plan for the day and know what you want to see then stick to your guns and find a driver who will give you a good price to take you where you want to go. Sometimes drivers try to convince you that you don't want to go to the place you have planned and that you should go somewhere else. Maybe they are right, and you are missing something special that you should see, but it could also be because their mum owns the beach bar, or it's just a shorter journey so they can be back for another fare nice and quickly! If you have done your research and have a plan, then don't be afraid to stick to it! That's not to say you shouldn't leave a bit of room for spontaneity on occasion, and some people really like just to busk the whole thing. You could ask a taxi driver for a price for his time, rather than for a distance; ask how much for the whole or maybe a half day and then get the driver to show you what he thinks you should see locally. This can be a success if you are in a small group (definitely NOT if you're on your own) and haven't done any planning. If you have no idea of what you want to see, there is no doubt that you could fall across some wonderful experiences, but it is not an approach I've personally had huge success with so far!

The important thing about all the planning you have done is that you have thought about it before you arrived. This might be the port where you're filling every minute with culture or the one where you are off to swim with the dolphins. This might be the day where actually you just want to do a bit of shopping and get back on board for a nice leisurely lunch and a massage in the spa. Whatever you want to do, it's your holiday, make the most of it!

CHAPTER 7

TRAVEL SAFELY
AVOIDING TROUBLE ASHORE

The main purpose of this chapter is not to scare you but to sound a note of caution about some of the things that can very occasionally go wrong. It is impossible to give specific advice, that would depend on the exact port you were visiting, but a little general advice could make your day ashore significantly safer. Cruise ship travel is statistically the safest way to see the world, but it does parachute you straight into areas that may be much poorer or more lawless than you are used to. Walking off your pristine air-conditioned ship that is full of smiling helpful people and straight out onto a hot, smelly dockside may take more than a moment to adjust to! There are areas around all ports, but particularly large industrial ones, that are really quite unsavoury, and in my opinion these are best avoided altogether. There will always be people who will want to walk in and out of port, but when it is well outside the main tourist area, my advice would always be to take a shuttle or taxi directly to the nicer parts of town. You really won't miss anything!

In general, my best advice is to **stay alert** and not to lose the common sense that you use to survive at home every day. Being on holiday does not give you any magical protection! Just as at home you should always take heed of local **security warnings**, and if there are any about a port (particularly if an announcement is made that solo travel is not advised) then listen and take note of what is said. This situation arose recently in Cozumel, Mexico when only escorted tour groups were allowed to leave the port and individual passengers were strongly advised against it. The implications to the local economy of making an announcement like that will have been seriously considered as it can quickly tarnish a port's reputation.

Once you are ashore, usual sensible advice applies – you wouldn't get into an unmarked minicab at home after all! There is usually a taxi wrangler in the cruise terminal with a board showing suggested prices for trips to various destinations. It's unlikely you will be able to negotiate down very much from these with another cab, and using the taxi desk to arrange a regular cabbie will mean that you know that you are using a reputable driver, and also that the taxi wrangler knows that they have taken passengers. If you can't find a taxi manager, then ask for advice from tourist information. Always fix a price beforehand or take a cab with a meter.

When you go ashore, try to look like a **traveller, not a tourist.** That may sound silly, but walking ashore in December wearing shorts, vest top, and a sun hat makes you an obvious target in a city where the locals are wrapped up in leather jackets, jeans, a scarf and boots. It may be the Mediterranean, it may be warmer than it is at home, but it still is not summer! Carry as little with you as possible – obviously, this will vary depending on what you are planning to do that day, but make sure you read Chapter 6 and really think about what you actually need to have with you. Do not walk off the ship with your cruise card dangling from a lanyard where everyone can see it, tuck it inside your shirt or into your bag. Don't stand in the middle of the town square reading a guidebook or looking at your map while your bag is hanging open by your side, just be sensible! Go and sit on a bench or in a cafe while you decide what you're going to do next. Always **walk confidently** and as if you know exactly where you're going, especially if you don't! Look and be alert.

If you are on a group tour, put your cruise tour number sticker inside your shirt or even inside your bag so that it's still available when needed, but isn't visible as soon as you walk into a shop. This is the sort of thing that you will mark you out as 'rich' by local standards and drive prices up everywhere you go! People worry about travelling alone when in port and prefer the security of a tour, but funnily enough ship's or other large group tours are more likely to be targeted by pickpockets. This is because a large group tends to move quite slowly and feel more secure but in fact is a target when crowding around a guide to hear information and are generally more easily distracted by a small incident or pushed through by a local without being alerted to potential pilfering.

Think about the **bag** you take ashore with you, avoid cruise ship logos for example. A cross body bag is safer and less easily grabbed than a bag hanging from your shoulder or held in your hand. In some parts on the world, bag snatching is a problem, for example, in Naples Italy, there are reports of pillion passengers on the back of a scooter leaning out to grab bag from your shoulder or hand as they whiz past. I always try and walk against the traffic for this reason or carry shopping in my hand away from the road. In crowded areas such as buses or trains switch your **backpack** round to the front to prevent someone from opening any pockets and removing items. Always wear your **camera** around your neck or put your hand through the strap and then wrap it around your wrist so that it can't easily be pulled out of your hand.

In bars or restaurants do not put your camera or bag on the back of your chair. A good piece of advice is to put the leg of your chair through a bag strap and then place it between your feet (although even then, we have heard stories of children crawling under tables to open bags). If you can keep your bag across your body or on your lap that will be safest. Avoid leaving bags or phones on the edge of the table while you eat especially if your table is by a road. Don't leave drinks unattended in case someone slips something into it, be careful just as you would at home. If you suddenly start feeling sleepy or giddy do not automatically assume that it is the sun or that you have overdone it, immediately tell someone else in your group that you feel funny and do not go anywhere alone. Try a short sit in the shade and some rehydration (Coke is good in an emergency) but if you start to feel worse ask someone to take you straight back to the ship.

Don't travel with all your money and cards in one place, spread it across different pockets, bags and purses. Spreading it around means that you don't have to open a wallet stuffed full of cash for the smallest purchase. A small amount of money that is easily available is sensible when you're buying small things, for instance in a busy market.

Many men use a money belt or wrap an elastic band around their wallet, which apparently makes it much more difficult for someone to remove from their pocket and the safest place for it is in an inside pocket or front trouser pocket, both of which are hardest for pickpockets to access.

If you use a separate wallet for travel, it will be much thinner and easier to conceal than your normal wallet as you need to have so much less in it. If you take your usual wallet or purse, then you should empty it right out before you go away. It contains many things that, whilst no use on holiday, would be a huge help to a thief intent on identity fraud. Remove everything that you will not need abroad such as an NHS or social security card, debit or store credit cards, work ID, gym ID, loyalty cards, library cards, discount cards, and also the things that you would really miss but would have no value to anyone else; receipts, credit notes, personal photos. None of this needs to be with you at all, and yet it would cause you a lot of grief to lose it especially because it could make it easier to steal your identity. When you take all of that out of your wallet and find that it is now so thin that everything else wants to fall out, you will see why I prefer to have a separate travel wallet! Some people advocate using a decoy or fake wallet with some expired credit cards and leftover currency from a previous trip in it that does not actually have any value to anybody. I'm not really sure that it is worth it, but you could consider the idea.

If you keep a list of emergency contacts in your wallet or bag then put a little thought into making it understandable to yourself alone (for example use initials rather than writing 'mum') as you do hear of people losing their wallet, and then later a relative getting a phone call saying 'your son is in prison in the Caribbean and you need to transfer money for his bail'. If you are sitting happily out of contact on your cruise ship that could be very distressing for those targeted.

If you take valuables ashore with you, then wear them! Keep your Rolex on your wrist when you go into the sea. If you put it in a shoe, cover it with a towel, and hope for the best, it may well be gone, along with your shoe, when you get back.

Be aware of well-practised distraction techniques; a drink being split on your arm or a sudden fight breaking out, shouting, or a crowd of kids running towards you are all a sign to immediately hold very tight to your possessions. A crowd intently watching a street performer like a magician or juggler could provide good cover for a group of pickpockets. Children playing and running through the crowd is a good sign to watch out for. A smart young woman asking you to complete a survey on local tourism may well be rummaging through your bag beneath her clipboard.

Being on holiday does not insulate you from fraudsters either; be particularly aware if you are buying a camera, expensive lens, or electronics in a shop. Make sure you see the assistant put the item you examined into the box or bag. If they go to get you a 'new one' make sure to open the box before leaving the shop. There are many, many stories of people who buy a particular item for a very good price only to find, once they are back on the ship and open the box, that they have been given something completely different.

You are not immune from local laws when you are on holiday. This particularly applies to drink driving laws if you hire a car. Buying counterfeit items, drugs, or seashells can all be illegal; check for local regulations or just avoid. Beware of local attitudes to clothing or sexuality. The local attitude towards LGBTQ+ travellers may be less tolerant in some parts of the world than the freedom that is expected at home. Transgender people in particular need to take specific advice on their itinerary as it can be illegal or cause huge difficulties to present as a different gender to that in your passport. This is best researched on specialist websites as you could find that the locally accepted modes of behaviour may mean that you prefer not to visit that country at all. In the main everyone has a great day ashore when they are on a cruise. If you are extremely unlucky and something should happen, then you need to consider the implications on your time of going to the police station to report the incident. You need to balance the cost of what you've lost against the cost of what it will mean if you miss the ship – you will find more about this in Chapter 9.

Serious crime is extremely unusual in tourist destinations, the local people and economy rely heavily on the goodwill of cruise passengers and the wider cruise industry. It is not helpful if their port gets a poor reputation and is marked out as a place that isn't safe to go. So you will normally only come across opportunistic, petty crime directed at property. If you take care of yours, then they will find someone else to target.

CHAPTER 8

ALL ABOARD
RETURNING TO THE SHIP

In contrast to the slight melancholy I feel at the end of a holiday, I am never particularly sad to leave a port and return to the ship after a day ashore. In fact, I think that one of the best things about cruising is that there is always something else to look forward to, even if it is just dinner! It is probably also because if I have really enjoyed somewhere, I know that there is always the option to plan a return on another cruise, for a weekend, or even for an actual holiday. My happiness to be back on board is in part because, although I am always super keen and excited to leave the ship in the morning, I generally start to think about getting back shortly after lunch! OK so that is a slight joke (we don't do lunch - see below!), but in truth, I am definitely not one of those people who is blasé about 'all aboard' times. You have probably already worked out from previous comments that I do not like to cut things fine at all!

Just another reminder about ships and local time at this point, as I mentioned previously the two are not always the same. The time that the ship will leave is shown on a sign at the gangway; this is in **ship's time.** If you don't normally use a watch but rely on your phone or a smartwatch for the time just be careful that it does not **update itself to local time** without you noticing when you connect to wifi or 4G! A low-tech ordinary watch that you can set as you want is quite useful on cruises.

The normal pattern of our days ashore is usually to **debark** (yes, it really is a word!) as early as possible, go to the **furthest part** of our planned itinerary, and then work our way back. We will normally stop for a drink and a snack (especially if we find a market or festival with street food), but I really cannot understand why people go ashore and then waste two hours having lunch! We tend to eat dinner quite late so getting back for a little afternoon tea and a sit by the pool is just perfect for me. Now you may want to come back aboard a little later than that but please truly consider and understand these words - **THE SHIP WILL LEAVE WITHOUT YOU!** If you think I am exaggerating then have a look on YouTube, there are lots of videos of people running after a ship, calling for it to come back! It is true that on occasion a ship might delay its departure for a while although that can work out to be very expensive for the cruise line - apparently an eight hour stop in Miami for the Harmony of the Seas costs more than $80,000, so if they were charged at that rate to wait another hour it would cost another $10,000! This is why 'the ship will wait for you' is untrue, as we discussed in Chapter 5, as it could well be cheaper for them to fly or bus your group to the next port. Sometimes it is not a financial consideration that means the ship absolutely has to leave at the scheduled time. To understand why, you need to know a little about how a cruise is planned.

A BIT OF NAUTICAL KNOW-HOW

The ship's course is plotted a couple of years ahead of the voyage taking place; it is actually considered at the same time as the itinerary is planned. Knowing that passengers can be transported between ports in the time allowed is a fairly important consideration before selling tickets for a cruise – makes sense really when you think about it. The ship's course is plotted using nautical charts (maps of the sea showing the depth of water, channels, and any obstacles to avoid) and it is the schedule that the Captain and crew are following. Nowadays charts are electronic, but there will always be a set of printed charts on the ship for emergencies. There is also a chart displayed somewhere on the ship for you to see. It is usually near the pool, often outside the entrance to the Buffet, if you can't find it just ask a crew member but definitely go and have a look.

So a chart shows the **minimum** depth of water (charts use a unit called fathoms, 1 is equal to about 6 feet) at given positions over a year but the **actual** depth under the ship varies from that because of the **tide**. This rise and fall of sea levels is caused by the combined effects of the gravitational pulls between the moon and sun combined with the effect of the rotation of the earth. So if all three are working together the difference in tide level over the day will be much greater than when they are working against each other. The time of day that the tide changes from rising to falling (or vice versa) is known as high or low tide. The direction that water is flowing in (the tide) reverses as well. High and Low Tide times and depths are not random; they can be calculated using the movement of the earth and stars, centuries ahead if you wanted! The results of these calculations are published as **tide tables**, and each major port has its own, calculated for its specific position on earth. The difference between the level of water at low and high tide in a particular place is known as its **tidal range**, and for many reasons, there is a huge variation in these across the world; in practical terms, this is why the steepness of the gangway can sometimes vary so much within a few hours. The difference in tidal ranges can be huge – in Piraeus, Greece it is only 0.10 metres but in Reykjavik, Iceland it is 4.86m. At St John's in Nova Scotia the range is 8.85m, but in the Bay of Fundy, just outside the harbour, the range reaches 16.00 metres!

So the bottom line is that this is known about in advance and planned for in the ship's course. The Captain knows how long it will take to travel to the next port and how much wriggle room he has. A delay could mean that the ship has to travel faster which would increase costs and potentially be less comfortable for passengers, but sometimes that is not an option because there is a specific point that has to be reached by an exact time, maybe a bridge that the ship needs to pass under at low tide or a particularly shallow section of ocean that it has to pass over close to high tide. The Captain will also know if there is bad weather forecast ahead of the ship and where the ship needs to be in relation to it. His **responsibility** is for the **safety and comfort** of the thousands of passengers who are on his ship, not the two idiots who are still in the souvenir shop or the bar on the pier! Bottom Line; never believe anyone who says the ship will wait unless it is the Captain himself!

'All aboard' is the time that the gangway is lifted, not the time you should plan to arrive back at port! Make sure you allow enough time to get back through the port to the ship as this can vary from almost half an hour to just a couple of minutes. It depends completely on the size of the port; you will be able to make an estimate about this as you leave in the morning but don't forget that you will also have **security** to pass through on the way back.

One of the reasons that it is hard to get specific information about larger ports is that the ship will rarely know, until they arrive, exactly which berth they will be allocated. This varies depending on what other ships are docked or expected and also on the level of security in force within the port; that will depend on **threat level** that the port has in operation that day. We once docked at Civitavecchia where we were surprised to find ourselves at the very furthest part of the harbour wall, especially since we were the only ship in port! It turned out that the local threat level was judged to be 'severe', so obviously, the ship was safest away from the town and the port entrance. Increased security also meant that taxis and private transfers were banned from approaching the ship, so the queue for the **shuttle bus** was large and slow, the alternative being a long hot walk along the empty pier. In industrial ports passengers are not allowed to walk around at all, you will always have to be dropped at the gate to join the port shuttle. If you are using a shuttle service you should plan to get back reasonably early as the last hour of people fighting for their place in the queue and onto the bus can be truly awful (we once witnessed some absolutely shocking behaviour in Zeebrugge where cruise passengers pushed over a security barrier so that they could barge their way onto the shuttle).

Similarly, in a tender port I would absolutely try to avoid the **last tender** of the day (details of which are shown where you leave it in the morning) as again, by then there doesn't seem to be a lot of what my mum used to call 'holiday spirit' in evidence! If you have to take a shuttle bus or tender I would definitely plan to be back early and spend some time on board. The ship will be quiet, and although the shops and Casino will be closed the bars, coffee shops and buffet will be open! The spa and pool area will be relatively empty, and it is surprising how much warmer it feels on deck when the ship isn't moving!

Thankfully in most cruise ports you can just walk through the terminal to get back on board, and things are a lot more civilised. You will know from the morning how much is available in the terminal and whether you want to leave yourself time to visit the rum shop or the jewellery concessions. Just as you did at the start of the cruise, you will have to pass through airport-style security scanners to reach the ship, in addition to passing through the onboard security checks and scanners.

It is probably obvious, but just worth making clear, that you can come and go from the ship throughout the day as you wish. It is an option to spend the morning ashore, come back for lunch and then go out again later and some ship's tours are only half a day long for this reason. It is also worth mentioning that it is fine for you to board at a different time from your travel companion, which is extremely useful if you want to send your other half back on board with the wet towels and snorkels while you mooch around the duty-free! Spending a little time in the terminal shops is fine but if you spot all the ship's excursion coaches arriving back I strongly advise that you move quickly to get yourself into the queue for security ahead of them!

After passing through port security you walk to your ship; now it may sound ridiculous, but please make sure that you know the name of your ship as it is not unusual for two ships from the same cruise line to be in port together. It is quite funny to witness the moment that people suddenly realise that they are in the wrong queue! Assuming you have the right ship you are safe once you reach the foot of the gangway, even if you are running late – breathe! There is normally a shady, tented area with a few seats set up at the foot of the ship's gangway where a couple of waiters will offer offering cold water/warm soup (itinerary dependant!) and sometimes cold flannels or warm blankets (ditto). The ubiquitous hand sanitiser will be prominent, and they will expect you to use it before joining the ship. The boarding process itself is run by **ship's security** who will visually check your cruise card (and send anyone queuing for the wrong ship across to the one on the other side of the quay!) and control the queue to avoid a buildup of people on the gangway itself for obvious safety reasons. If you need to get back on board urgently for any reason, speak to one of the waiters and take a seat there, while they liaise with Security to get you back on board. Just a word of warning, it is never sensible to say that you feel sick or ill in an attempt to jump a long queue to board. Any hint of real sickness will require a consultation with the ship's **medical team**. If they are concerned that you could be contagious or are seriously unwell, then they may decide you should be hospitalised and left behind in the port, either for your own well-being or in order to prevent the spread of disease aboard. Do not ever argue with ships security; they are the **ship's police force**, they have unlimited powers on behalf of the Captain as well as to confine you to the Brig; the ship's prison cells.

As you enter the ship your card will be scanned, your identity checked again, and your possessions passed through a security scanner. If you have bought anything ashore that is not allowed to be brought on board, then it will be confiscated. The list of **banned items** is the same as was in your original cruise information; it is also displayed on posters in this area. Obviously, this includes weapons of any kind (including those for martial arts), explosives, stun guns and ammunition which would be confiscated for safety reasons, along with knives with a blade longer than 4 inches, handcuffs, and replica firearms. Also chemicals, shells, candles, incense sticks, and other flammable items. Bottles of alcohol are not normally allowed to be brought on board, even for your own consumption, and neither are drugs **even if they are legal to buy or use in that port**. This is not airport security-style confiscation which means you will never see your purchases again so stay calm! Security will very politely take your cruise card to log the offending items in and will give them all back to you as you leave the ship at the end of the cruise. As I just said... 'Do not ever argue with ship's security; they are the ship's police force.'.

The queue for the lifts is normally pretty bad as not all the lifts in the ship will come down all the way down to the bottom level. Obviously many people have to use them but if you are able it is always best to walk up, even just to the Atrium level where there are other lifts to choose from.

And finally, unless the next day will be a **sea day**, you should take the chance to pop to Guest Services and begin your enquiries for tomorrow!

CHAPTER 9

SOS

WHAT TO DO IF THINGS GO WRONG

This chapter is fairly short, and that is because hopefully the advice I have given you throughout the book, but in particular in Chapter 7, will mean that it is redundant! Things can and will happen that are outside of your control, but in essence, my default advice is:

1. Get back to the ship, if you can.
2. Contact the Port Agent for help, if you cannot.

This is not just to do with missing the ship through lateness but also in the event of a crime, personal attack, local unrest, or illness. In any serious situation, you need to contact the Port Agent as soon as possible to explain what is happening so that they can support you as best they can. You may initially be put in direct contact with the ship so that you can stay in touch for advice but once the ship has left port, the Port Agent will be your only point of contact.

Missing the ship through lateness is a really big error, if it happens through your own mistake or bad planning (and that would include heavy traffic or getting lost), then you probably would not be covered by your travel insurance. You would have to pay for any costs incurred in catching up with the ship. Obviously, nobody thinks they will miss the ship, and nobody intends to do so – it is so easy to say "Oh that won't happen to us" but the thing that causes you a problem may be completely out of your control. Traffic, accidents, and sudden illness can all cause trouble, and you really should factor in a reasonable time for a certain level of unexpected delay.

If a motorway is closed due to an accident or all trains are suddenly cancelled then try and gather as much evidence as you can to support a claim on your insurance later. A photo from your smartphone with a time stamp showing that you were at the station in plenty of time but that the sign is showing cancellations, or a screenshot of Google maps with the only road to the port closed would be a help. Do not forget that any photos on your smartphone will be time stamped which can be a big help. We once had a tour guide who didn't leave a town that was two hours away from the port until an hour and a half before the ship was scheduled to leave! I thought my screenshots and photos would help with our insurance claim, but luckily the ship waited. They did turn out to be invaluable in writing a serious letter of complaint though, and it got us (and many others in our group) a full refund! DO NOT WASTE TIME gathering evidence when you could be using it to move! Only consider it if you have time; the most important thing is to get as quickly as possible back to the ship.

If you miss the ship at the start of your holiday the same advice applies. If you are travelling on transport booked through the ship, they will organise your transfer to the next port. If you arrive just as the ship leaves call the Emergency Contact number given in your boarding instructions **immediately**, as occasionally it is possible to arrange your transfer using the boat going out to collect the ship's pilot (this is an option that I never, ever want to explore!).

Crime can happen anywhere and being on a cruise does not insulate you from it. If you are unfortunate enough to be affected then what you should do will depend on the seriousness of the incident. In general, if I were able to get back on board and sail away, I would do so. I would prefer to deal with the aftermath such as making a statement to the police through the ship's communications system or by Skype rather than staying alone in a country where I had just been the victim of a crime. Obviously, we all want to help the police and prevent the same thing happening to others, but I would rather do that from a place of safety. If, for example, you have had your bag stolen or you have been attacked, then you will need to report this to the local police so that they can investigate and give you a crime report for your insurance, but it is not worth missing the ship for. If you are distressed or upset, you need to be where you feel safe. If something happens in the early part of the day, then you could ask someone to call the Port Agent for you and take his advice. It is possible that they would send someone from the ship to support you and to make sure you get back on time. However, if something happens later in the day then just get back to the ship. Go through security and right to the gangway, explain as soon as you arrive what has happened and ask them to call the Head of Security, he will help you deal with it from there.

In the case of an accident it would really depend on how serious it is – if you are ok to get into a taxi, I would still say return to the ship and go to see the medical team there. If they advise you that you have to go to hospital, then they will arrange your transfer. This would be as a last resort as they will try to keep you on board if at all possible. If they feel that you need more specialist treatment then at least you will have the chance to ask someone to pack a bag for you. If you are unable to walk, or are so unwell or badly injured that you have to be transported to hospital by ambulance, then ask someone to call the Port Agent immediately.

In case of terrorism or local unrest, you must follow any local advice you are given and do whatever seems safest at the time. If you are sheltering somewhere safe and it would be dangerous to leave then try and contact the Port Agent for advice. At the end of the day, you are better missing the ship from a place of safety than being killed or injured en-route to the port. In those circumstances, there will be other passengers affected too, and the Port Agent will work to bring you all together and get you out safely. The ship would delay its departure as long as possible unless that would put the ship itself in danger. The Captain is responsible for both the ship and its passengers, and sometimes that is the sort of difficult choice he would have to make.

Enough - we don't want to think about such things! Let's just go ashore with a plan of what we are doing and the Port Agents details from the daily schedule in our bag. We will try to look like travellers, not tourists, keep out of dangerous areas, stay alert, and be safe. That way everyone will enjoy a great cruise with some wonderful portExploring!

CHAPTER 10

TIME TO GO HOME
THE END OF YOUR CRUISE

Sigh! So that's it, we are reaching the end of planning your cruise but stick with me for one last chapter as I have some ideas about how to end the cruise in style, maybe even with a smile on your face!

One awesome idea that you could consider is just not getting off the ship at all! If you have no time constraints and a very large sense of adventure you could always ask Guest Services about their bookings for the following week, because if they still have availability at this late stage, you might get an extremely good deal, either to keep your stateroom for a second week or even for an upgrade! I have been told unofficially that the bigger your onboard spend, or the larger your losses at the casino, the more likely it is that they will do you some sort of deal and keep you on board. We are not actually advocating gambling or drinking as a money saving idea, but it is something that could be useful to know. Adding on a second cruise like this is known as **back to back** cruising and, because cruises often run on a two-week cycle, the chances are that you would have a completely different itinerary from the one you had just done. However, now you are a *Confident portExplorer*, you know that after spending an hour or two in an internet cafe you will have put together some exciting plans for your new ports! Even if you returned to some of the same ports again, you could repurpose some of the plans that you discarded back in Chapter 4, but which are still sitting in your trusty notebook, and have a great time! Now obviously this option relies a lot on the flexibility of your travel plans but even flight tickets can be rescheduled and sometimes it is great to make a truly spontaneous decision. It makes me think of the quote from Helen Keller, *"Life is either a daring adventure or nothing at all"*.

TOP TIP

If transfers are included, you will only get one per destination. If you are travelling AIRPORT - HOTEL - SHIP choose 'airport to hotel' as your included transfer, but for SHIP - HOTEL - AIRPORT choose to include 'ship to hotel'. This is because airports and cruise terminals often operate a Fixed Price Taxi fare into town, which is substantially more expensive than the standard cab fare for the reverse journey.

Maybe making this sort of decision at such a late stage is a bit too spontaneous for most people but it could be worth considering in the weeks leading up to your cruise when you could potentially find get some really good deals. Some people even get off one cruise ship and straight onto another one, sometimes even onto a different cruise line; one quick trip to the laundry and off you go again!

Sadly, most of us have limited holidays and can only dream of the day we retire and can cruise hop like that, but when you are planning your holiday it definitely is worth thinking about trying to extend your holiday with a post-cruise hotel stay, maybe overnight or slightly longer – two or three days is probably enough to ease you gently back into the real world. This is particularly sensible if you are flying a long way to begin your cruise, as otherwise you are in danger of not seeing the 'home' city other than from a taxi on the way to and from the airport! Cruise lines can often source very good deals with the local hotels they use for their overnight stays, and they will be able to organise flights to coincide with your changed dates, at the original cruise price as long as the flights were scheduled (not charter) flights and that any alterations are made at the time of booking.

Another thing you might consider booking in advance that could brighten your homeward journey is an upgraded flight; leaving the ship but spending a few hours in business class lounges and seats definitely softens the blow of leaving and keeps the holiday going just a little longer...

If you haven't managed to wangle a back to back cruise, then it is time to plan how to leave the ship and think about the logistics of how you are going to get off! As I have said before this book is really focused on planning your time ashore, and you will find much more about planning related to the actual cruise in *The Confident Cruiser,* but let's just quickly cover the most important things you DO need to have done before you finally leave the ship. By the evening before you should have...

1. Confirmed or checked in for any flights.
2. Made any **future cruise deposits** or reservations, as the office will not be open on the final morning (A future cruise deposit can be used with a booking made

in any way, i.e., direct with the cruise line, a discount site, or with your usual TA).

3. Registered a **credit card** to pay your onboard account automatically and so avoid the queue on the last morning.

4. **Checked** your onboard account early enough to miss the huge queue of people with queries at Customer Services. We try to check it every day as oddly if you pick up a few mistakes at the beginning of a cruise, they seem to stop happening so much.

5. Collected your **passports** or had them delivered back to you, normally after the last port of call if they were being held by the ship.

6. **Emptied** your safe!

The schedule for departing guests gets delivered to your cabin a couple of days before the end of the cruise. You will have been given luggage tags and allocated a particular timed departure slot. The colour of those tags designates the time you leave in the morning as well as the matching coloured zone in the luggage hall where you will find your cases once you are off the ship. It is worth knowing that these slots are not set in stone, and you can often negotiate an alternative with Guest Services, especially if you have a good enough reason to change or you are trying to move your departure to a later time slot. It's worth knowing that passengers who are taking all their own luggage with them, as well as Elite and Suite passengers, can pretty much leave when they want to. If you have booked a morning **cruise transfer** to the airport or a final day combined cruise **excursion/**

transfer with the cruise line, you put your bags out in the normal way the night before, pick them up from the luggage hall and take them to the coaches yourself. If you have a **private transfer** or other DIY onward travel, you do the same. An afternoon or evening cruise transfer will require you to take your bags to a holding room on board (normally a conference room, somewhere near the theatre) and collect them later before boarding your coach. This is so that they don't get muddled with the bags coming onto the ship and it's a great way to avoid having to sit around with your bags all day. Plus, it's an excellent reason for always booking cruise flights/transfers and/or excursions for the final day. If you are doing this, it is best to have lockable hand baggage to leave on board, which will be much safer than spending your final portExploring day carrying your passport, cards and documents around with you. Your cruise card will be valid until you have collected your bags and disembarked. Coming back to the ship you should follow signs for **transit passengers** to avoid getting muddled in with the new arrivals.

Packing to go home needs a little more thinking about than you might expect, especially if you are flying. Whatever colour tags you have been given, your main suitcases will need to put out for collection on your final evening, usually by about 23.00, but check the instructions. A few years ago the routine was that people put their bags out and went down to dinner in the clothes they were travelling home in or they went back to their cabin early, packed their evening wear, put their suitcases outside and went to bed. Bars and music would close down early on the last night to encourage early nights all round, but today this is much less likely to happen, especially on lines such as MSC that run on a pretty continuous loop with people getting on and off at almost every port. The best plan is to put your main suitcases out before dinner, and have wheeled hand baggage that can take your clothes from your last night, your night stuff, and toiletries (see below). Check you have your **complete outfit** ready for the next day, especially shoes, **before** putting your suitcases out for collection. There is always someone who has to leave the ship in stilettos and a sparkly dress which is not a great look in a port at 08.00 in the morning!

Just a couple of points about packing that are particularly relevant to flights. Don't forget to check the weight of your cases as you would normally - I usually have a **luggage scale** with me, but if you don't then your cabin steward will probably be able to find one for you somewhere. You need to remember that normal hand baggage rules will apply in relation to sharp objects, your wash-bag, makeup, and in particular to **liquids**. I still mourn a bottle of perfume from the ships duty-free that was confiscated at check in. It was still sealed in its box, so in my head, it was the same as a bottle bought in the airport, but the security officer at the airport thought otherwise and wouldn't allow it onto the plane with me! Talking of security, you need to remember that you will get back any items that were confiscated during the cruise as you reach the gangway for the last time. You will need to have a bag available to hold them as you walk down to the luggage hall (security generally just gives you the bottle!) and you also need to have left some space for them in your main suitcase. The bottles of alcohol, pocket knives, and candles that weren't allowed on board won't be allowed in your hand baggage either so you will have to do a little repacking once you collect your case. I strongly suggest that you do it straight away, at the side of the luggage hall, before you take the bags out to the transfer coach as it will be much easier than trying to do it at the airport.

When the time comes to **leave the ship** try not to be carrying too much, it can be a real nuisance if you have to wait around in lounges waiting for your colour departure tag to be called. You leave your stateroom usually by 08.00 and then go to have breakfast (the main dining room is much less of a bun fight than the buffet!) while you wait for your group to be called for disembarkation. Leaving the ship for the last time is a bit of an anti-climax, the same routine of checking your card that you have done at every port, a beep, a quick goodbye and you are off the ship. You can keep your cruise card as a souvenir, but it will never work again, it's very sad!

So hopefully you have had a wonderful time on your cruise holiday. You've loved the ship, the food, the people you met, the dancing, the shows, and the wonderful crew but most importantly for me, you've enjoyed every single day that you have spent ashore. I hope you've balanced excitement, culture, local colour, and history with a bit of relaxation and that you haven't exhausted yourself so much that you need another holiday to recover. It really is worth taking the time to make some final notes, maybe on the journey home, in your trusty notebook. Think about what went well and what you wish you'd done differently, as this notebook now forms a valuable record of every aspect of your cruise. It will be invaluable when you come to plan the next one - and that's the last thing I have to tell you; cruising is addictive. There will always be another cruise to think about, and you will never stop planning what you want to do on the next one. Happy portExploring!